Selected Stories by
ALEXANDRE DUMAS

Books in this Series:

Selected Stories by O. Henry
Selected Stories by Anton Chekhov
Selected Stories by Guy de Maupassant
Selected Stories by Mark Twain
Selected Stories by Edgar Allan Poe
Selected Stories by Rudyard Kipling
Selected Stories by Saki
Selected Stories by Oscar Wilde
Selected Stories by Honoré de Balzac
Selected Stories by Charles Dickens
Selected Stories by D.H. Lawrence
Selected Stories by H.G. Wells
Selected Stories by Jack London
Selected Stories by Joseph Conrad
Selected Stories by Leo Tolstoy
Selected Stories by Sir Arthur Conan Doyle
Selected Stories by James Joyce
Selected Stories by Virginia Woolf
Selected Stories by Thomas Hardy
Selected Stories by Fyodor Dostoyevsky
Selected Stories by Katherine Mansfield
Selected Stories by Wilkie Collins
Selected Stories by Robert Louis Stevenson
Selected Stories by Howard Pyle
Selected Stories by Jerome K. Jerome
Selected Stories by Sir Walter Scott
Selected Stories by H. Rider Haggard
Selected Stories by G.K. Chesterton
Selected Stories by Bram Stoker
Selected Stories by Henry James
Selected Stories by F. Scott Fitzgerald
Selected Stories by W.W. Jacobs
Selected Stories by A.A. Milne
Selected Stories by Nathaniel Hawthorne

Selected Stories by
ALEXANDRE DUMAS

Published by
Rupa Publications India Pvt. Ltd 2015
7/16, Ansari Road, Daryaganj
New Delhi 110002

Sales Centres:
Allahabad Bengaluru Chennai
Hyderabad Jaipur Kathmandu
Kolkata Mumbai

Selection and Introduction copyright © Terry O'Brien 2015

All rights reserved.
No part of this publication may be reproduced, transmitted,
or stored in a retrieval system, in any form or by any means,
electronic, mechanical, photocopying, recording or otherwise,
without the prior permission of the publisher.

ISBN: 978-81-291-3723-4

First impression 2015

10 9 8 7 6 5 4 3 2 1

Printed at Shree Maitrey Printech Pvt. Ltd., Noida

This book is sold subject to the condition that it shall not,
by way of trade or otherwise, be lent, resold, hired out, or otherwise
circulated, without the publisher's prior consent, in any form of binding or
cover other than that in which it is published.

CONTENTS

Introduction vii

1　A Bal Masqué　　　　　　　　　　　　　　　　1

2　Solange　　　　　　　　　　　　　　　　　　11

3　The Cenci　　　　　　　　　　　　　　　　　29

4　The Countess De Saint-Geran　　　　　　　　67

INTRODUCTION

Alexandre Dumas (24 July 1802–5 December 1870) was one of the most prolific and popular French writers of the nineteenth century. He is best known for his historical novels of high adventure.

Alexandre Dumas began his career as a highly successful playwright, and later moved to writing novels, rewriting one of his plays as his first serial novel, *Le Capitaine Paul*. He founded a production studio in 1838 where he oversaw the writing of several stories. He wrote some of his best-known works, including *The Count of Monte Cristo* and *The Three Musketeers*, in collaboration with Auguste Maquet.

From 1839 to 1841, he collaborated with several friends to compile *Celebrated Crimes*, a collection of essays on crime and well-known criminals in eight volumes. In 1861, he founded and published *L'Indipendente*, a newspaper supporting Italian unification. His encyclopaedia, *Grand Dictionnaire de Cuisine*, was published in 1873 after his death.

His last and unfinished work, *The Knight of Sainte-Hermine*, was completed by Claude Schopp. It was published in English translation as *The Last Cavalier*.

This collection is a selection from the best of his short fiction.

- In 'A Bal Masqué' a man narrates to his friend the tragic story of a mysterious young woman.

- 'Solange' is a dark haunting story that takes place during the French Revolution. A romance, it is a story without a happy ending.
- 'The Cenci' is a gruesome tale of incest, murder and intrigue in the Cenci family.
- 'The Countess De Saint-Geran' recounts the story behind the lawsuit contesting the claims of the Countess de Saint-Geran's child and rightful heir.

1

A BAL MASQUÉ

I said that I was in to no one; one of my friends forced admission.

My servant announced Mr. Anthony R——. Behind Joseph's livery I saw the corner of a black redingote; it is probable that the wearer of the redingote, from his side, saw a flap of my dressing gown; impossible to conceal myself.

'Very well! Let him enter,' I said out loud. 'Let him go to the Devil,' I said to myself.

While working it is only the woman you love who can disturb you with impunity, for she is always at bottom interested in what you are doing.

I went up to him, therefore, with the half-bored face of an author interrupted in one of those moments of sorest self-mistrust, while I found him so pale and haggard that the first words I addressed to him were these:

'What is the matter? What has happened to you?'

'Oh! Let me take breath,' said he. 'I'm going to tell you all about it, besides, it's a dream perhaps, or perhaps I am mad.'

He threw himself into an armchair, and let his head drop between his hands.

I looked at him in astonishment; his hair was dripping with rain; his shoes, his knees, and the bottom of his trousers were covered with mud. I went to the window; I saw at the door his servant and his cabriolet; I could make nothing out of it all.

He saw my surprise.

'I have been to the cemetery of Pére-Lachaise,' said he.

'At ten o'clock in the morning?'

'I was there at seven—cursed bal masqué!'

I could not imagine what a bal masqué and Pére-Lachaise had to do with one another. I resigned myself, and turning my back to the mantelpiece began to roll a cigarette for him between my fingers with the phlegm and the patience of a Spaniard.

While he was coming to the point I hinted to Anthony that I, for my part, was commonly very susceptible to attentions of that kind.

He made me a sign of thanks, but pushed my hand away.

Finally I bent over to light the cigarette for myself: Anthony stopped me.

'Alexandre,' he said to me. 'Listen, I beg of you.'

'But you have been here already a quarter of an hour and have not told me anything.'

'Oh! it is a most strange adventure.'

I got up, placed my cigarette on the mantelpiece and crossed my arms like a man resigned; only I began to believe, as he did, that he was fast becoming mad.

'You remember the ball at the Opéra, where I met you?' he said to me after a moment's silence.

'The last one where there were at least two hundred people?'

'The very same. I left you with the intention of abandoning myself to one of those varieties of which they spoke to me as being a curiosity even in the midst of our curious times; you wished to dissuade me from going; a fatality drove me on. Oh, you! why did you not see it all, you who have the knack of observation? Why were not Hoffman or Callot there to paint the picture as the fantastic, burlesque thing kept unrolling itself beneath my eyes? Unsatisfied and in melancholy mood I walked away, about to quit the Opéra; I came to a hall that was overflowing and in high spirits: corridors, boxes, parterre. Everything was obstructed. I made a tour of the room; twenty masks called me by name and told me theirs. These were all leaders—aristocrats and merchants—in the undignified disguise of pierrots, of postilions, of merry-andrews, or of fishwives. They were all young people of family, of culture, of talent; and there, forgetful of family, talent, breeding, they were resurrecting in the midst of our sedate and serious times a soiree of the Regency. They had told me about it, and yet I could not have believed it!—I mounted a few steps and leaning against a pillar, half hidden by it, I fixed my eyes on that sea of human beings surging beneath me. Their dominoes, of all colors, their motley costumes, their grotesque disguises formed a spectacle resembling nothing human. The music began to play. Oh, it was then these gargoyle creatures stirred themselves to the sound of that orchestra whose harmony reached me only in the midst of cries, of laughs, of hootings; they hung on to each other by their hands, by their arms, by their necks; a long coil formed itself, beginning with a circular motion, the dancers, men and women, stamping with their feet, made the dust break forth with a noise, the atoms of which were rendered visible by the wan light of the lustres; turning at ever-increasing speed with bizarre postures, with unseemly gestures, with cries full of abandonment; turning always faster and still faster, swaying and swinging like drunken men, yelling like lost women, with more delirium than delight, with more passion than pleasure; resembling a coil of the damned doing infernal penance under the scourge of demons! All this passed beneath my eyes, at my feet. I felt the wind of their whirling past; as they rushed by each one whom I knew flung a word at me that made me blush. All this noise, all this humming, all this confusion, all this music went on in my brain as well as in the room! I soon came to the point of no longer knowing whether that which I had before my eyes was a dream or reality; I came to the point of asking myself whether it was not I who was mad and they who were sane; I was seized with a weird temptation to throw myself into the midst of this pandemonium, like Faust through the Witches' Sabbath, and I felt that I too, would then have cries, postures, laughs like theirs. Oh! from that to madness there is but one step. I was appalled; I flung myself out of the room, followed even to the street door by shrieks that were like those cries of passion that come out of the caverns of the fallow deer.

'I stopped a moment under the portico to collect myself; I did not wish to venture into the street; with such confusion still in my soul I might not be able to find my way; I might, perhaps, be thrown under the wheels of some carriage I had not seen coming. I was as a drunken man might be who begins to recover sufficient reason in his clouded brain to recognize his condition, and who, feeling the will return but not the power, with fixed eyes and staring, leans motionless against some street post or some tree on the public promenade.

'At that moment a carriage stopped before the door, a woman alighted or rather shot herself from the doorway.

'She entered beneath the peristyle, turning her head from right to left like one who had lost her way; she was dressed in a black domino, had her face covered by a velvet mask. She presented herself at the door.

'"Your ticket," said the door-keeper.

'"My ticket?" she replied. "I have none."

'"Then get one at the box-office."

'The domino came back under the peristyle, fumbled nervously about in all her pockets.

'"No money!" she cried. "Ah! this ring—a ticket of admission for this ring," she said.

"'Impossible,' replied the woman who was distributing the cards. 'We do not make bargains of that kind.'

'And she pushed away the brilliant, which fell to the ground and rolled to my side.

'The domino remained still without moving, forgetting the ring, sunk in thought.

'I picked up the ring and handed it to her.

'Through her mask I saw her eyes fixed on mine.

"'You must help me to get in,' she said to me; 'You must, for pity's sake.'

"'But I am going out, madame,' I said to her.

"'Then give me six francs for this ring, and you will render me a service for which I shall bless you my life long.'

'I replaced the ring on her finger; I went to the box-office, I took two tickets. We reentered together.

'As we arrived within the corridor I felt that she was tottering. Then with her second hand she made a kind of ring around my arm.

"'Are you in pain?' I asked her.

"'No, no, it is nothing,' she replied, 'a dizziness, that is all—'

'She hurried me into the hall.

'We reentered into that giddy Charenton.

'Three times we made the tour, breaking our way with great difficulty through the waves of masks that were hurling themselves one upon the other; she trembling at every unseemly word that came to her ear; I blushing to be seen giving my arm to a woman who would thus put herself in the way of such words; then we returned to the end of the hall.

'She fell upon a sofa. I remained standing in front of her, my hand leaning on the back of her seat.

"'Oh! this must seem to you very bizarre,' she said, 'but not more so than to me, I swear to you. I have not the slightest idea of all this' (she looked at the ball), 'for even in my dreams I could not imagine such things. But they wrote me, you see, that he would be here with a woman, and what sort of a woman should it be who could come to a place like this?"

'I made a gesture of surprise; she understood.

'"But *I* am here, you wish to ask, do you not? Oh! but for me that is another thing: I, I am looking for him; I, I am his wife. As for these people, it is madness and dissipation that drives them hither. But I, I, it is jealousy infernal! I have been everywhere looking for him; I have been all night in a cemetery; I have been at Grève on the day of an execution; and yet, I swear to you, as a young girl I have never once gone into the street without my mother; as a wife I have never taken one step out of doors without being followed by a lackey; and yet here I am, the same as all these women who are so familiar with the way; here I am giving my arm to a man whom I do not know, blushing under my mask at the opinion he ought to have of me! I know all this! Have you ever been jealous, monsieur?"

'"Unhappily," I replied to her.

'"Then you will forgive me, for you understand. You know that voice that cries out to you 'Do!' as in the ear of a madman; you have felt that arm that pushes one into shame and crime, like the arm of fate. You know that at such a moment one is capable of everything, if one can only get vengeance."

'I was about to reply; all at once she rose, her eyes fastened on two dominoes that were passing in front of us at that moment.

'"Silence!" she said.

'And she hurried me on following in their footsteps. I was thrown into the middle of an intrigue of which I understood nothing; I could feel all the threads vibrating, but could take hold of none of them by the end; but this poor wife seemed so troubled that she became interesting. I obeyed like a child, so imperious is real feeling, and we set ourselves to follow the two masks, one of which was evidently a man, the other a woman. They spoke in a low voice; the sounds reached our ears with difficulty.

'"It is he!" she murmured; "it is his voice; yes, yes, that is his figure—"

'The latter of the two dominoes began to laugh.

'"That is his laugh," said she; "it is he, monsieur, it is he! The letter said true, O, mon Dieu, mon Dieu!"

'In the mean while the two masks kept on, and we followed them always. They went out of the hall, and we went out after them; they took the stairs leading to the boxes, and we ascended in their footsteps; they did not stop till they came to the boxes in the centre; we were like their two shadows. A little closed box was opened; they entered it; the door again closed upon them.

'The poor creature I was supporting on my arm frightened me by her excitement. I could not see her face, but crushed against me as she was, I could feel her heart beating, her body shivering, her limbs trembling. There was something uncanny in the way there came to me such knowledge of unheard-of suffering, the spectacle of which I had before my very eyes, of whose victim I knew nothing, and of the cause of which I was completely ignorant. Nevertheless, for nothing in this world would I have abandoned that woman at such a moment.

'As she saw the two masks enter the box and the box close upon them, she stopped still a moment, motionless, and as if overwhelmed. Then she sprang forward to the door to listen. Placed as she was her slightest movement would betray her presence and ruin her; I dragged her back violently by the arm, I lifted the latch of the adjoining box, I drew her in after me, I lowered the grille and pulled the door to.

'"If you wish to listen," I said to her, "at least listen from here."

'She fell upon one knee and flattened her ear against the partition, and I—I held myself erect on the opposite side, my arms crossed, my head bent and thoughtful.

'All that I had been able to observe of that woman seemed to me to indicate a type of beauty. The lower part of her face, which was not concealed by her mask, was youthful, velvety, and round; her lips were scarlet and delicate; her teeth, which the black velvet mask falling just above them made appear still whiter, were small, separated, and glistening; her hand was one to be modeled, her figure to be held between the fingers; her black hair, silky, escaped in profusion from beneath the hood of her domino, and the foot of a child, that played in and out under her skirt, looked as if it should have trouble in balancing her body, all lithe, all graceful, all airy as it was. Oh! what a marvelous piece of perfection must she be! Oh! he that should hold her in his arms, that should see every faculty of that spirit absorbed in loving him, that should feel the beating of her heart against his, her tremblings, her nervous palpitations, and that should be able to say: "All of this, all of this, comes of love, of love for me, for me alone among all the millions of men, for me, angel predestined! Oh! that man!—that man!—"

'Such were my thoughts, when all at once I saw that woman rise, turn toward me, and say to me in a voice broken and fierce:

'"Monsieur, I am beautiful, I swear it; I am young, I am but nineteen. Until now I have been white as an angel of the Creation—ah, well—" she threw both arms about my neck, "—ah, well, I am yours—take me!—"

'At the same instant I felt her lips pressed close to mine, and the effect of a bite, rather than that of a kiss, ran shuddering and dismayed through my whole body; over my eyes passed a cloud of flame.

'Ten minutes later I was holding her in my arms, in a swoon, half dead and sobbing.

'Slowly she came to herself; through her mask I made out how haggard were her eyes; I saw the lower part of her pale face, I heard her teeth chatter one upon the other, as in the chill of a fever. I see it all once more.

'She remembered all that had taken place, and fell at my feet.

'"If you have any compassion," she said to me, sobbing, "any pity, turn away your eyes from me, never seek to know me; let me go and forget me. I will remember for two!"

'At these words she rose again; quickly, like a thought that escapes us, she darted toward the door, opened it, and coming back again, "Do not follow me, in heaven's name, Monsieur, do not follow me!" she said.

'The door pushed violently open, closed again between her and me, stole her from my sight, like an apparition. I have never seen her more!

'I have never seen her more! And ever since, ever since the six months that have glided by, I have sought her everywhere, at balls, at spectacles, at promenades. Every time I have seen from a distance a woman with lithe figure, with a foot like a child's, with black hair, I have followed her, I have drawn near to her, I have looked into her face, hoping that her blushes would betray her. Nowhere have I found her again, in no place have I seen her again—except at night, except in my dreams! Oh! there, there she reappears; there I feel her, I feel her embraces, her biting caresses so ardent, as if she had something of the devil in her; then the mask has fallen and a face most grotesque appeared to me at times blurred, as if veiled in a cloud; sometimes brilliant, as if circled by an aureole; sometimes pale, with a skull white and naked, with eyes vanished from the orbits, with teeth chattering and few. In short, ever since that night, I have ceased to live; burning with mad passion for a woman I do not know, hoping always and always disappointed at my hopes. Jealous without the right to be so, without knowing of whom to be jealous, not daring to avow such madness, and all the time pursued, preyed upon, wasted away, consumed by her.'

As he finished these words he tore a letter from his breast.

'Now that I have told you everything,' he said to me, 'take this letter and read it.'

I took the letter and read:

'Have you perhaps forgotten a poor woman who has forgotten nothing and who dies because she can not forget?

'When you receive this letter I shall be no more. Then go to the cemetery of Pére-Lachaise, tell the concierge to let you see among the newest graves one that bears on its stone the simple name "Marie," and when you are face to face with that grave, fall on your knees and pray.'

'Ah, well!' continued Anthony, 'I received that letter yesterday, and I went there this morning. The concierge conducted me to the grave, and I remained two hours on my knees there, praying and weeping. Do you understand? She was there, that woman. Her flaming spirit had stolen away; the body consumed by it had bowed, even to breaking, beneath the burden of jealousy and of remorse; she was there, under my feet, and she had lived, and she had died, for me unknown; unknown!—and taking a place in my life as she had taken one in the grave; unknown!—and burying in my heart a corpse, cold and lifeless, as she had buried one in the sepulchre—Oh! Do you know anything to equal it? Do you know any event so appalling? Therefore, now, no more hope. I will see her again never. I would dig up her grave that I might recover, perhaps, some traces wherewithal to reconstruct her face; and I love her always! Do you understand, Alexandre? I love her like a madman; and I would kill myself this instant in order to rejoin her, if she were not to remain unknown to me for eternity, as she was unknown to me in this world.'

With these words he snatched the letter from my hands, kissed it over and over again, and began to weep like a little child.

I took him in my arms, and not knowing what to say to him, I wept with him.

2

SOLANGE

Leaving l'Abbaye, I walked straight across the Place Turenne to the Rue Tournon, where I had lodgings, when I heard a woman scream for help.

It could not be an assault to commit robbery, for it was hardly ten o'clock in the evening. I ran to the corner of the place whence the sounds proceeded, and by the light of the moon, just then breaking through the clouds, I beheld a woman in the midst of a patrol of sans-culottes.

The lady observed me at the same instant, and seeing, by the character of my dress, that I did not belong to the common order of people, she ran toward me, exclaiming:

'There is M. Albert! He knows me! He will tell you that I am the daughter of Mme. Ledieu, the laundress.'

With these words the poor creature, pale and trembling with excitement, seized my arm and clung to me as a shipwrecked sailor to a spar.

'No matter whether you are the daughter of Mme. Ledieu or some one else, as you have no pass, you must go with us to the guard-house.'

The young girl pressed my arm. I perceived in this pressure the expression of her great distress of mind. I understood it.

'So it is you, my poor Solange?' I said. 'What are you doing here?'

'There, messieurs!' she exclaimed in tone of deep anxiety; 'do you believe me now?'

'You might at least say "citizens!"'

'Ah, sergeant, do not blame me for speaking that way,' said the pretty young girl; 'my mother has many customers among the great people, and taught me to be polite. That's how I acquired this bad habit—the habit of the aristocrats; and, you know, sergeant, it's so hard to shake off old habits!'

This answer, delivered in trembling accents, concealed a delicate irony that was lost on all save me. I asked myself, who is this young woman? The mystery seemed complete. This alone was clear: she was not the daughter of a laundress.

'How did I come here, Citizen Albert?' she asked. 'Well, I will tell you. I went to deliver some washing. The lady was not at home, and so I waited; for in these hard times every one needs what little money is coming to him. In that way it grew dark, and so I fell among these gentlemen—beg pardon, I would say citizens. They asked for my pass. As I did not have it with me, they were going to take me to the guard-house. I cried out in terror, which brought you to the scene; and as luck would have it, you are a friend. I said to myself, as M. Albert knows my name to be Solange Ledi300, he will vouch for me; and that you will, will you not, M. Albert?'

'Certainly, I will vouch for you.'

'Very well,' said the leader of the patrol; 'and who, pray, will vouch for you, my friend?'

'Danton! Do you know him? Is he a good patriot?'

'Oh, if Danton will vouch for you, I have nothing to say.'

'Well, there is a session of the Cordeliers to-day. Let us go there.'

'Good,' said the leader. 'Citizens, let us go to the Cordeliers.'

The club of the Cordeliers met at the old Cordelier monastery in the Rue l'Observance. We arrived there after scarce a minute's walk. At the door I tore a page from my note-book, wrote a few words upon it with a lead pencil, gave it to the sergeant, and requested him to hand it to Danton, while I waited outside with the men.

The sergeant entered the clubhouse and returned with Danton.

'What!' said he to me; 'they have arrested you, my friend? You, the friend of Camilles—you, one of the most loyal republicans? Citizens,' he continued, addressing the sergeant, 'I vouch for him. Is that sufficient?'

'You vouch for him. Do you also vouch for her?' asked the stubborn sergeant.

'For her? To whom do you refer?'

'This girl.'

'For everything; for everybody who may be in his company. Does that satisfy you?'

'Yes,' said the man; 'especially since I have had the privilege of seeing you.'

With a cheer for Danton, the patrol marched away. I was about to thank Danton, when his name was called repeatedly within.

'Pardon me, my friend,' he said; 'you hear? There is my hand; I must leave you—the left. I gave my right to the sergeant. Who knows, the good patriot may have scrofula?'

'I'm coming!' he exclaimed, addressing those within in his mighty voice with which he could pacify or arouse the masses. He hastened into the house.

I remained standing at the door, alone with my unknown.

'And now, my lady,' I said, 'whither would you have me escort you? I am at your disposal.'

'Why, to Mme. Ledieu,' she said with a laugh. 'I told you

she was my mother.'

'And where does Mme. Ledieu reside?'

'Rue Ferou, 24.'

'Then, let us proceed to Rue Ferou, 24.'

On the way neither of us spoke a word. But by the light of the moon, enthroned in serene glory in the sky, I was able to observe her at my leisure. She was a charming girl of twenty or twenty-two—brunette, with large blue eyes, more expressive of intelligence than melancholy—a finely chiseled nose, mocking lips, teeth of pearl, hands like a queen's, and feet like a child's; and all these, in spite of her costume of a laundress, betokened an aristocratic air that had aroused the sergeant's suspicions not without justice.

Arrived at the door of the house, we looked at each other a moment in silence.

'Well, my dear M. Albert, what do you wish?' my fair unknown asked with a smile.

'I was about to say, my dear Mlle. Solange, that it was hardly worth while to meet if we are to part so soon.'

'Oh, I beg ten thousand pardons! I find it was well worth the while; for if I had not met you, I should have been dragged to the guard-house, and there it would have been discovered that I am not the daughter of Mme. Ledieu—in fact, it would have developed that I am an aristocrat, and in all likelihood they would have cut off my head.'

'You admit, then, that you are an aristocrat?'

'I admit nothing.'

'At least you might tell me your name.'

'Solange.'

'I know very well that this name, which I gave you on the inspiration of the moment, is not your right name.'

'No matter; I like it, and I am going to keep it—at least for you.'

'Why should you keep it for me, if we are not to meet again?'

'I did not say that. I only said that if we should meet again it will not be necessary for you to know my name any more than that I should know yours. To me you will be known as Albert, and to you I shall always be Solange.'

'So be it, then; but I say, Solange,' I began.

'I am listening, Albert,' she replied.

'You are an aristocrat—that you admit.'

'If I did not admit it, you would surmise it, and so my admission would be divested of half its merit.'

'And you were pursued because you were suspected of being an aristocrat?'

'I fear so.'

'And you are hiding to escape persecution?'

'In the Rue Ferou, No. 24, with Mme. Ledieu, whose husband was my father's coachman. You see, I have no secret from you.'

'And your father?'

'I shall make no concealment, my dear Albert, of anything that relates to me. But my father's secrets are not my own. My father is in hiding, hoping to make his escape. That is all I can tell you.'

'And what are you going to do?'

'Go with my father, if that be possible. If not, allow him to depart without me until the opportunity offers itself to me to join him.'

'Were you coming from your father when the guard arrested you to-night?'

'Yes.'

'Listen, dearest Solange.'

'I am all attention.'

'You observed all that took place to-night?'

'Yes. I saw that you had powerful influence.'

'I regret my power is not very great. However, I have friends.'

'I made the acquaintance of one of them.'

'And you know he is not one of the least powerful men of the times.'

'Do you intend to enlist his influence to enable my father to escape?'

'No, I reserve him for you.'

'But my father?'

'I have other ways of helping your father.'

'Other ways?' exclaimed Solange, seizing my hands and studying me with an anxious expression.

'If I serve your father, will you then sometimes think kindly of me?'

'Oh, I shall all my life hold you in grateful remembrance!'

She uttered these words with an enchanting expression of devotion. Then she looked at me beseechingly and said:

'But will that satisfy you?'

'Yes,' I said.

'Ah, I was not mistaken. You are kind, generous. I thank you for my father and myself. Even if you should fail, I shall be grateful for what you have already done!'

'When shall we meet again, Solange?'

'When do you think it necessary to see me again?'

'To-morrow, when I hope to have good news for you.'

'Well, then, to-morrow.'

'Where?'

'Here.'

'Here in the street?'

'Well, mon Dieu!' she exclaimed. 'You see, it is the safest place. For thirty minutes, while we have been talking here, not a soul has passed.'

'Why may I not go to you, or you come to me?'

'Because it would compromise the good people if you should come to me, and you would incur serious risk it I should go to you.'

'Oh, I would give you the pass of one of my relatives.'

'And send your relative to the guillotine if I should be accidentally arrested!'

'True. I will bring you a pass made out in the name of Solange.'

'Charming! You observe Solange is my real name.'

'And the hour?'

'The same at which we met to-night—ten o'clock if you please.'

'All right; ten o'clock. And how shall we meet?'

'That is very simple. Be at the door at five minutes of ten, and at ten I will come down.'

'Then, at ten to-morrow, dear Solange.'

'To-morrow at ten, dear Albert.'

I wanted to kiss her hand; she offered me her brow.

The next day I was in the street at half past nine. At a quarter of ten Solange opened the door. We were both ahead of time.

With one leap I was by her side.

'I see you have good news,' she said.

'Excellent! First, here is a pass for you.'

'First my father!'

She repelled my hand.

'Your father is saved, if he wishes.'

'Wishes, you say? What is required of him?'

'He must trust me.'

'That is assured.'

'Have you seen him?'

'Yes.'

'You have discussed the situation with him?'

'It was unavoidable. Heaven will help us.'

'Did you tell your father all?'

'I told him you had saved my life yesterday, and that you would perhaps save his to-morrow.'

'To-morrow! Yes, quite right; to-morrow I shall save his life, if it is his will.'

'How? What? Speak! Speak! If that were possible, how fortunately all things have come to pass!'

'However—' I began hesitatingly.

'Well?'

'It will be impossible for you to accompany him.'

'I told you I was resolute.'

'I am quite confident, however, that I shall be able later to procure a passport for you.'

'First tell me about my father; my own distress is less important.'

'Well, I told you I had friends, did I not?'

'Yes.'

'To-day I sought out one of them.'

'Proceed.'

'A man whose name is familiar to you; whose name is a guarantee of courage and honor.'

'And this man is?'

'Marceau.'

'General Marceau?'

'Yes.'

'True, he will keep a promise.'

'Well, he has promised.'

'Mon Dieu! How happy you make me! What has he promised? Tell me all.'

'He has promised to help us.'

'In what manner?'

'In a very simple manner. Kléber has just had him promoted to the command of the western army. He departs to-morrow night.'

'To-morrow night! We shall have no time to make the smallest preparation.'

'There are no preparations to make.'

'I do not understand.'

'He will take your father with him.'

'My father?'

'Yes, as his secretary. Arrived in the Vendée, your father will pledge his word to the general to undertake nothing against France. From there he will escape to Brittany, and from Brittany to England. When he arrives in London, he will inform you; I shall obtain a passport for you, and you will join him in London.'

'To-morrow,' exclaimed Solange; 'my father departs to-morrow!'

'There is no time to waste.'

'My father has not been informed.'

'Inform him.'

'To-night?'

'To-night.'

'But how, at this hour?'

'You have a pass and my arm.'

'True. My pass.'

I gave it to her. She thrust it into her bosom.

'Now, your arm.'

I gave her my arm, and we walked away. When we arrived at the Place Turenne—that is, the spot where we had met the night before—she said: 'Await me here.'

I bowed and waited.

She disappeared around the corner of what was formerly the Hôtel Malignon. After a lapse of fifteen minutes she returned.

'Come,' she said, 'my father wishes to receive and thank you.'

She took my arm and led me up to the Rue St. Guillaume, opposite the Hôtel Mortemart. Arrived here, she took a bunch of keys from her pocket, opened a small, concealed door, took me by the hand, conducted me up two flights of steps, and knocked in a peculiar manner.

A man of forty-eight or fifty years opened the door. He was dressed as a working man and appeared to be a book-binder. But at the first utterance that burst from his lips, the evidence of the seigneur was unmistakable.

'Monsieur,' he said, 'Providence has sent you to us. I regard you an emissary of fate. Is it true that you can save me, or, what is more, that you wish to save me?'

I admitted him completely to my confidence. I informed him that Marceau would take him as his secretary, and would exact no promise other than that he would not take up arms against France.

'I cheerfully promise it now, and will repeat it to him.'

'I thank you in his name as well as in my own.'

'But when does Marceau depart?'

'To-morrow.'

'Shall I go to him to-night?'

'Whenever you please; he expects you.'

Father and daughter looked at each other.

'I think it would be wise to go this very night,' said Solange.

'I am ready; but if I should be arrested, seeing that I have no permit?'

'Here is mine.'

'But you?'

'Oh, I am known.'

'Where does Marceau reside?'

'Rue de l'Université, 40, with his sister, Mlle. Dégraviers-Marceau.'

'Will you accompany me?'

'I shall follow you at a distance, to accompany mademoiselle home when you are gone.'

'How will Marceau know that I am the man of whom you spoke to him?'

'You will hand him this tri-colored cockade; that is the sign of identification.'

'And how shall I reward my liberator?'

'By allowing him to save your daughter also.'

'Very well.'

He put on his hat and extinguished the lights, and we descended by the gleam of the moon which penetrated the stair-windows.

At the foot of the steps he took his daughter's arm, and by way of the Rue des Saints Pères we reached Rue de l'Université. I followed them at a distance of ten paces. We arrived at No. 40 without having met any one. I rejoined them there.

'That is a good omen,' I said; 'do you wish me to go up with you?'

'No. Do not compromise yourself any further. Await my daughter here.'

I bowed.

'And now, once more, thanks and farewell,' he said, giving me his hand: 'Language has no words to express my gratitude. I pray that heaven may some day grant me the opportunity of giving fuller expression to my feelings.'

I answered him with a pressure of the hand.

He entered the house. Solange followed him; but she, too, pressed my hand before she entered.

In ten minutes the door was reopened.

'Well?' I asked.

'Your friend,' she said, 'is worthy of his name; he is as kind and considerate as yourself. He knows that it will contribute to my happiness to remain with my father until the moment of departure. His sister has ordered a bed placed in her room. To-morrow at three o'clock my father will be out of danger. To-morrow evening at ten I shall expect you in the Rue Ferou, if the gratitude of a daughter who owes her father's life to you is worth the trouble.'

'Oh, be sure I shall come. Did your father charge you with any message for me?'

'He thanks you for your pass, which he returns to you, and begs you to join him as soon as possible.'

'Whenever it may be your desire to go,' I said, with a strange sensation at my heart.

'At least, I must know where I am to join him,' she said. 'Ah, you are not yet rid of me!'

I seized her hand and pressed it against my heart, but she offered me her brow, as on the previous evening, and said: 'Until to-morrow.'

I kissed her on the brow; but now I no longer strained her hand against my breast, but her heaving bosom, her throbbing heart.

I went home in a state of delirious ecstasy such as I had never experienced. Was it the consciousness of a generous action, or was it love for this adorable creature? I know not whether I slept or woke. I only know that all the harmonies of nature were singing within me; that the night seemed endless, and the day eternal; I know that though I wished to speed the time, I did not wish to lose a moment of the days still to come.

The next day I was in the Rue Ferou at nine o'clock. At half-past nine Solange made her appearance.

She approached me and threw her arms around my neck.

'Saved!' she said; 'my father is saved! And this I owe you. Oh, how I love you!'

Two weeks later Solange received a letter announcing her father's safe arrival in England.

The next day I brought her a passport.

When Solange received it she burst into tears.

'You do not love me!' she exclaimed.

'I love you better than my life,' I replied; 'but I pledged your father my word, and I must keep it.'

'Then, I will break mine,' she said. 'Yes, Albert; if you have the heart to let me go, I have not the courage to leave you.'

Alas, she remained!

Three months had passed since that night on which we talked of her escape, and in all that time not a word of parting had passed her lips.

Solange had taken lodgings in the Rue Turenne. I had rented them in her name. I knew no other, while she always addressed me as Albert. I had found her a place as teacher in a young ladies' seminary solely to withdraw her from the espionage of the revolutionary police, which had become more scrutinizing than ever.

Sundays we passed together in the small dwelling, from the bedroom of which we could see the spot where we had first met. We exchanged letters daily, she writing to me under the name of Solange, and I to her under that of Albert.

Those three months were the happiest of my life.

In the meantime I was making some interesting experiments suggested by one of the guillotiniers. I had obtained permission to make certain scientific tests with the bodies and heads of those who perished on the scaffold. Sad to say, available subjects were not wanting. Not a day passed but thirty or forty persons were guillotined, and blood flowed so copiously on the Place de la Révolution that it became necessary to dig a trench three feet deep around the scaffolding. This trench was covered with deals. One of them loosened under the feet of an eight-year-old lad, who fell into the abominable pit and was drowned.

For self-evident reasons I said nothing to Solange of the studies that occupied my attention during the day. In the beginning my occupation had inspired me with pity and loathing, but as time wore on I said: 'These studies are for the good of humanity,' for I hoped to convince the law-makers of the wisdom of abolishing capital punishment.

The Cemetery of Clamart had been assigned to me, and all the heads and trunks of the victims of the executioner had been placed at my disposal. A small chapel in one corner of the cemetery had been converted into a kind of laboratory for my benefit. You know, when the queens were driven from the palaces, God was banished from the churches.

Every day at six the horrible procession filed in. The bodies were heaped together in a wagon, the heads in a sack. I chose some bodies and heads in a haphazard fashion, while the remainder were thrown into a common grave.

In the midst of this occupation with the dead, my love for Solange increased from day to day; while the poor child reciprocated my affection with the whole power of her pure soul.

Often I had thought of making her my wife; often we had mutually pictured to ourselves the happiness of such a union. But in order to become my wife, it would be necessary for Solange to reveal her name; and this name, which was that of an emigrant, an aristocrat, meant death.

Her father had repeatedly urged her by letter to hasten her departure, but she had informed him of our engagement. She had requested his consent, and he had given it, so that all had gone well to this extent.

The trial and execution of the queen, Marie Antoinette, had plunged me, too, into deepest sadness. Solange was all tears, and we could not rid ourselves of a strange feeling of despondency, a presentiment of approaching danger, that compressed our hearts. In vain I tried to whisper courage to Solange. Weeping, she reclined in my arms, and I could not comfort her, because my own words lacked the ring of confidence.

We passed the night together as usual, but the night was even more depressing than the day. I recall now that a dog, locked up in a room below us, howled till two o'clock in the morning. The next day we were told that the dog's master had gone away with the key in his pocket, had been arrested on the way, tried at three, and executed at four.

The time had come for us to part. Solange's duties at the school began at nine o'clock in the morning. Her school was in the vicinity of the Botanic Gardens. I hesitated long to let her go; she, too, was loath to part from me. But it must be. Solange was prone to be an object of unpleasant inquiries.

I called a conveyance and accompanied her as far as the Rue des Fosses-Saint-Bernard, where I got out and left her to pursue her way alone. All the way we lay mutely wrapped in each other's arms, mingling tears with our kisses.

After leaving the carriage, I stood as if rooted to the ground. I heard Solange call me, but I dared not go to her, because her face, moist with tears, and her hysterical manner were calculated to attract attention.

Utterly wretched, I returned home, passing the entire day in writing to Solange. In the evening I sent her an entire volume of love-pledges.

My letter had hardly gone to the post when I received one from her.

She had been sharply reprimanded for coming late; had been subjected to a severe cross-examination, and threatened with forfeiture of her next holiday. But she vowed to join me even at the cost of her place. I thought I should go mad at the prospect of being parted from her a whole week. I was more depressed because a letter which had arrived from her father appeared to have been tampered with.

I passed a wretched night and a still more miserable day.

The next day the weather was appalling. Nature seemed to be dissolving in a cold, ceaseless rain—a rain like that which announces the approach of winter. All the way to the laboratory my ears were tortured with the criers announcing the names of the condemned, a large number of men, women, and children. The bloody harvest was over-rich. I should not lack subjects for my investigations that day.

The day ended early. At four o'clock I arrived at Clamart; it was almost night.

The view of the cemetery, with its large, new-made graves; the sparse, leafless trees that swayed in the wind, was desolate, almost appalling.

A large, open pit yawned before me. It was to receive to-day's harvest from the Place de la Révolution. An exceedingly large number of victims was expected, for the pit was deeper than usual.

Mechanically I approached the grave. At the bottom the water had gathered in a pool; my feet slipped; I came within an inch of falling in. My hair stood on end. The rain had drenched me to the skin. I shuddered and hastened into the laboratory.

It was, as I have said, an abandoned chapel. My eyes searched—I know not why—to discover if some traces of the holy purpose to which the edifice had once been devoted did not still adhere to the walls or to the altar; but the walls were bare, the altar empty.

I struck a light and deposited the candle on the operating-table on which lay scattered a miscellaneous assortment of the strange instruments I employed. I sat down and fell into a reverie. I thought of the poor queen, whom I had seen in her beauty, glory, and happiness, yesterday carted to the scaffold, pursued by the execrations of a people, to-day lying headless on the common sinners' bier—she who had slept beneath the gilded canopy of the throne of the Tuileries and St. Cloud.

As I sat thus, absorbed in gloomy meditation, wind and rain without redoubled in fury. The rain-drops dashed against the window-panes, the storm swept with melancholy moaning through the branches of the trees. Anon there mingled with the violence of the elements the sound of wheels.

It was the executioner's red hearse with its ghastly freight from the Place de la Révolution.

The door of the little chapel was pushed ajar, and two men, drenched with rain, entered, carrying a sack between them.

'There, M. Ledru,' said the guillotinier; 'there is what your heart longs for! Be in no hurry this night! We'll leave you to enjoy their society alone. Orders are not to cover them up till to-morrow, and so they'll not take cold.'

With a horrible laugh, the two executioners deposited the sack in a corner, near the former altar, right in front of me. Thereupon they sauntered out, leaving open the door, which swung furiously on its hinges till my candle flashed and flared in the fierce draft.

I heard them unharness the horse, lock the cemetery, and go away.

I was strangely impelled to go with them, but an indefinable power fettered me in my place. I could not repress a shudder. I had no fear; but the violence of the storm, the splashing of the rain, the whistling sounds of the lashing branches, the shrill vibration of the atmosphere, which made my candle tremble— all this filled me with a vague terror that began at the roots of my hair and communicated itself to every part of my body.

Suddenly I fancied I heard a voice! A voice at once soft and plaintive; a voice within the chapel, pronouncing the name of 'Albert!'

I was startled.

'Albert!'

But one person in all the world addressed me by that name!

Slowly I directed my weeping eyes around the chapel, which, though small, was not completely lighted by the feeble rays of the candle, leaving the nooks and angles in darkness, and my look remained fixed on the blood-soaked sack near the altar with its hideous contents.

At this moment the same voice repeated the same name, only it sounded fainter and more plaintive.

'Albert!'

I bolted out of my chair, frozen with horror.

The voice seemed to proceed from the sack!

I touched myself to make sure that I was awake; then I walked toward the sack with my arms extended before me, but stark and staring with horror. I thrust my hand into it. Then it seemed to me as if two lips, still warm, pressed a kiss upon my fingers!

I had reached that stage of boundless terror where the excess of fear turns into the audacity of despair. I seized the head and, collapsing in my chair, placed it in front of me.

Then I gave vent to a fearful scream. This head, with its lips still warm, with eyes half closed, was the head of Solange!

I thought I should go mad.

Three times I called:

'Solange! Solange! Solange!'

At the third time she opened her eyes and looked at me. Tears trickled down her cheeks, then a moist glow darted from her eyes, as if the soul were passing, and the eyes closed, never to open again.

I sprang to my feet a raving maniac. I wanted to fly; I knocked against the table; it fell. The candle was extinguished; the head rolled upon the floor, and I fell prostrate, as if a terrible fever had stricken me down—an icy shudder convulsed me, and, with a deep sigh, I swooned.

The following morning at six the grave-diggers found me, cold as the flagstones on which I lay.

Solange, betrayed by her father's letter, had been arrested the same day, condemned, and executed.

The head that had called me, the eyes that had looked at me, were the head, the eyes, of Solange!

3

THE CENCI

Should you ever go to Rome and visit the villa Pamphili, no doubt, after having sought under its tall pines and along its canals the shade and freshness so rare in the capital of the Christian world, you will descend towards the Janiculum Hill by a charming road, in the middle of which you will find the Pauline fountain. Having passed this monument, and having lingered a moment on the terrace of the church of St. Peter Montorio, which commands the whole of Rome, you will visit the cloister of Bramante, in the middle of which, sunk a few feet below the level, is built, on the identical place where St. Peter was crucified, a little temple, half Greek, half Christian; you will thence ascend by a side door into the church itself. There, the attentive cicerone will show you, in the first chapel to the right, the Christ Scourged, by Sebastian del Piombo, and in the third chapel to the left, an Entombment by Fiammingo; having examined these two masterpieces at leisure, he will take you to each end of the transverse cross, and will show you—on one side a picture by Salviati, on slate, and on the other a work by Vasari; then, pointing out in melancholy tones a copy of Guido's Martyrdom of St. Peter on the high altar, he will relate to you how for three centuries the divine Raffaelle's Transfiguration was worshipped in that spot; how it was carried away by the French in 1809, and restored to the pope by the Allies in 1814. As you have already in all probability admired this masterpiece in the Vatican, allow him to expatiate, and search at the foot of the altar for a mortuary slab, which you will identify by a cross and the single word, Orate; under this gravestone is buried Beatrice Cenci, whose tragic story cannot but impress you profoundly.

She was the daughter of Francesco Cenci. Whether or not it be true that men are born in harmony with their epoch, and that some embody its good qualities and others its bad ones, it may nevertheless interest our readers to cast a rapid glance over the period which had just passed when the events which we are about to relate took place. Francesco Cenci will then appear to them as the diabolical incarnation of his time.

On the 11th of August, 1492, after the lingering death-agony of Innocent VIII, during which two hundred and twenty murders were committed in the streets of Rome, Alexander VI ascended the pontifical throne. Son of a sister of Pope Calixtus III, Roderigo Lenzuoli Borgia, before being created cardinal, had five children by Rosa Vanozza, whom he afterwards caused to be married to a rich Roman. These children were:

Francis, Duke of Gandia;

Caesar, bishop and cardinal, afterwards Duke of Valentinois;

Lucrezia, who was married four times: her first husband was Giovanni Sforza, lord of Pesaro, whom she left owing to his impotence; the second, Alfonso, Duke of Bisiglia, whom her brother Caesar caused to be assassinated; the third, Alfonso d'Este, Duke of Ferrara, from whom a second divorce separated her; finally, the fourth, Alfonso of Aragon, who was stabbed to death on the steps of the basilica of St. Peter, and afterwards, three weeks later, strangled, because he did not die soon enough from his wounds, which nevertheless were mortal;

Giofre, Count of Squillace, of whom little is known;

And, finally, a youngest son, of whom nothing at all is known.

The most famous of these three brothers was Caesar Borgia. He had made every arrangement a plotter could make to be King of Italy at the death of his father the pope, and his measures were so carefully taken as to leave no doubt in his own mind as to the success of this vast project. Every chance was provided against, except one; but Satan himself could hardly have foreseen this particular one. The reader will judge for himself.

The pope had invited Cardinal Adrien to supper in his vineyard on the Belvidere; Cardinal Adrien was very rich, and the pope wished to inherit his wealth, as he already had acquired that of the Cardinals of Sant' Angelo, Capua, and Modena. To effect this, Caesar Borgia sent two bottles of poisoned wine to his father's cup-bearer, without taking him into his confidence; he only instructed him not to serve this wine till he himself gave orders to do so; unfortunately, during supper the cup-bearer left his post for a moment, and in this interval a careless butler served the poisoned wine to the pope, to Caesar Borgia, and to Cardinal Corneto.

Alexander VI died some hours afterwards; Caesar Borgia was confined to bed, and sloughed off his skin; while Cardinal Corneto lost his sight and his senses, and was brought to death's door.

Pius III succeeded Alexander VI, and reigned twenty-five days; on the twenty-sixth he was poisoned also.

Caesar Borgia had under his control eighteen Spanish cardinals who owed to him their places in the Sacred College; these cardinals were entirely his creatures, and he could command them absolutely. As he was in a moribund condition and could make no use of them for himself, he sold them to Giuliano della Rovere, and Giuliano della Rovere was elected pope, under the name of Julius II. To the Rome of Nero succeeded the Athens of Pericles.

Leo X succeeded Julius II, and under his pontificate Christianity assumed a pagan character, which, passing from art into manners, gives to this epoch a strange complexion. Crimes for the moment disappeared, to give place to vices; but to charming vices, vices in good taste, such as those indulged in by Alcibiades and sung by Catullus. Leo X died after having assembled under his reign, which lasted eight years, eight months, and nineteen days, Michael Angelo, Raffaelle, Leonardo da Vinci, Correggio, Titian, Andrea del Sarto, Fra Bartolommeo, Giulio Romano, Ariosto, Guicciardini, and Macchiavelli.

Giulio di Medici and Pompeo Colonna had equal claims to succeed him. As both were skilful politicians, experienced courtiers, and moreover of real and almost equal merit, neither of them could obtain a majority, and the Conclave was prolonged almost indefinitely, to the great fatigue of the cardinals. So it happened one day that a cardinal, more tired than the rest, proposed to elect, instead of either Medici or Colonna, the son, some say of a weaver, others of a brewer of Utrecht, of whom no one had ever thought till then, and who was for the moment acting head of affairs in Spain, in the absence of Charles the Fifth. The jest prospered in the ears of those who heard it; all the cardinals approved their colleague's proposal, and Adrien became pope by a mere accident.

He was a perfect specimen of the Flemish type, a regular Dutchman, and could not speak a word of Italian. When he arrived in Rome, and saw the Greek masterpieces of sculpture collected at vast cost by Leo X, he wished to break them to pieces, exclaiming, 'Suet idola anticorum.' His first act was to despatch a papal nuncio, Francesco Cherigato, to the Diet of Nuremberg, convened to discuss the reforms of Luther, with instructions which give a vivid notion of the manners of the time.

'Candidly confess,' said he, 'that God has permitted this schism and this persecution on account of the sins of man, and especially those of priests and prelates of the Church; for we know that many abominable things have taken place in the Holy See.'

Adrien wished to bring the Romans back to the simple and austere manners of the early Church, and with this object pushed reform to the minutest details. For instance, of the hundred grooms maintained by Leo X, he retained only a dozen, in order, he said, to have two more than the cardinals.

A pope like this could not reign long: he died after a year's pontificate. The morning after his death his physician's door was found decorated with garlands of flowers, bearing this inscription: 'To the liberator of his country.'

Giulio di Medici and Pompeo Colonna were again rival candidates. Intrigues recommenced, and the Conclave was once more so divided that at one time the cardinals thought they could only escape the difficulty in which they were placed by doing what they had done before, and electing a third competitor; they were even talking about Cardinal Orsini, when Giulio di Medici, one of the rival candidates, hit upon a very ingenious expedient. He wanted only five votes; five of his partisans each offered to bet five of Colonna's a hundred thousand ducats to ten thousand against the election of Giulio di Medici. At the very first ballot after the wager, Giulio di Medici got the five votes he wanted; no objection could be made, the cardinals had not been bribed; they had made a bet, that was all.

Thus it happened, on the 18th of November, 1523, Giulio di Medici was proclaimed pope under the name of Clement VII. The same day, he generously paid the five hundred thousand ducats which his five partisans had lost.

It was under this pontificate, and during the seven months

in which Rome, conquered by the Lutheran soldiers of the Constable of Bourbon, saw holy things subjected to the most frightful profanations, that Francesco Cenci was born.

He was the son of Monsignor Nicolo Cenci, afterwards apostolic treasurer during the pontificate of Pius V. Under this venerable prelate, who occupied himself much more with the spiritual than the temporal administration of his kingdom, Nicolo Cenci took advantage of his spiritual head's abstraction of worldly matters to amass a net revenue of a hundred and sixty thousand piastres, about f32,000 of our money. Francesco Cenci, who was his only son, inherited this fortune.

His youth was spent under popes so occupied with the schism of Luther that they had no time to think of anything else. The result was, that Francesco Cenci, inheriting vicious instincts and master of an immense fortune which enabled him to purchase immunity, abandoned himself to all the evil passions of his fiery and passionate temperament. Five times during his profligate career imprisoned for abominable crimes, he only succeeded in procuring his liberation by the payment of two hundred thousand piastres, or about one million francs. It should be explained that popes at this time were in great need of money.

The lawless profligacy of Francesco Cenci first began seriously to attract public attention under the pontificate of Gregory XIII. This reign offered marvellous facilities for the development of a reputation such as that which this reckless Italian Don Juan seemed bent on acquiring. Under the Bolognese Buoncampagno, a free hand was given to those able to pay both assassins and judges. Rape and murder were so common that public justice scarcely troubled itself with these trifling things, if nobody appeared to prosecute the guilty parties. The good Gregory had his reward for his easygoing indulgence; he was spared to rejoice over the Massacre of St. Bartholomew.

Francesco Cenci was at the time of which we are speaking a man of forty-four or forty-five years of age, about five feet four inches in height, symmetrically proportioned, and very strong, although rather thin; his hair was streaked with grey, his eyes were large and expressive, although the upper eyelids drooped somewhat; his nose was long, his lips were thin, and wore habitually a pleasant smile, except when his eye perceived an enemy; at this moment his features assumed a terrible expression; on such occasions, and whenever moved or even slightly irritated, he was seized with a fit of nervous trembling, which lasted long after the cause which provoked it had passed. An adept in all manly exercises and especially in horsemanship, he sometimes used to ride without stopping from Rome to Naples, a distance of forty-one leagues, passing through the forest of San Germano and the Pontine marshes heedless of brigands, although he might be alone and unarmed save for his sword and dagger. When his horse fell from fatigue, he bought another; were the owner unwilling to sell he took it by force; if resistance were made, he struck, and always with the point, never the hilt. In most cases, being well known throughout the Papal States as a free-handed person, nobody tried to thwart him; some yielding through fear, others from motives of interest. Impious, sacrilegious, and atheistical, he never entered a church except to profane its sanctity. It was said of him that he had a morbid appetite for novelties in crime, and that there was no outrage he would not commit if he hoped by so doing to enjoy a new sensation.

At the age of about forty-five he had married a very rich woman, whose name is not mentioned by any chronicler. She died, leaving him seven children—five boys and two girls. He then married Lucrezia Petroni, a perfect beauty of the Roman type, except for the ivory pallor of her complexion. By this second marriage he had no children.

As if Francesco Cenci were void of all natural affection, he hated his children, and was at no pains to conceal his feelings towards them: on one occasion, when he was building, in the courtyard of his magnificent palace, near the Tiber, a chapel dedicated to St. Thomas, he remarked to the architect, when instructing him to design a family vault, 'That is where I hope to bury them all.' The architect often subsequently admitted that he was so terrified by the fiendish laugh which accompanied these words, that had not Francesco Cenci's work been extremely profitable, he would have refused to go on with it.

As soon as his three eldest boys, Giacomo, Cristoforo, and Rocco, were out of their tutors' hands, in order to get rid of them he sent them to the University of Salamanca, where, out of sight, they were out of mind, for he thought no more about them, and did not even send them the means of subsistence. In these straits, after struggling for some months against their wretched plight, the lads were obliged to leave Salamanca, and beg their way home, tramping barefoot through France and Italy, till they made their way back to Rome, where they found their father harsher and more unkind than ever.

This happened in the early part of the reign of Clement VIII, famed for his justice. The three youths resolved to apply to him, to grant them an allowance out of their father's immense income. They consequently repaired to Frascati, where the pope was building the beautiful Aldobrandini Villa, and stated their case. The pope admitted the justice of their claims, and ordered Francesco to allow each of them two thousand crowns a year. He endeavoured by every possible means to evade this decree, but the pope's orders were too stringent to be disobeyed.

About this period he was for the third time imprisoned for infamous crimes. His three sons then again petitioned the pope, alleging that their father dishonoured the family name, and praying that the extreme rigour of the law, a capital sentence, should be enforced in his case. The pope pronounced this conduct unnatural and odious, and drove them with ignominy from his presence. As for Francesco, he escaped, as on the two previous occasions, by the payment of a large sum of money.

It will be readily understood that his sons' conduct on this occasion did not improve their father's disposition towards them, but as their independent pensions enabled them to keep out of his way, his rage fell with all the greater intensity on his two unhappy daughters. Their situation soon became so intolerable, that the elder, contriving to elude the close supervision under which she was kept, forwarded to the pope a petition, relating the cruel treatment to which she was subjected, and praying His Holiness either to give her in marriage or place her in a convent. Clement VIII took pity on her; compelled Francesco Cenci to give her a dowry of sixty thousand crowns, and married her to Carlo Gabrielli, of a noble family of Gubbio. Francesco was driven nearly frantic with rage when he saw this victim released from his clutches.

About the same time death relieved him from two other encumbrances: his sons Rocco and Cristoforo were killed within a year of each other; the latter by a bungling medical practitioner whose name is unknown; the former by Paolo Corso di Massa, in the streets of Rome. This came as a relief to Francesco, whose avarice pursued his sons even after their death, for he intimated to the priest that he would not spend a farthing on funeral services. They were accordingly borne to the paupers' graves which he had caused to be prepared for them, and when he saw them both interred, he cried out that he was well rid of such good-for-nothing children, but that he should be perfectly happy only when the remaining five were buried with the first two, and that when he had got rid of the last he himself would burn down his palace as a bonfire to celebrate the event.

But Francesco took every precaution against his second daughter, Beatrice Cenci, following the example of her elder sister. She was then a child of twelve or thirteen years of age, beautiful and innocent as an angel. Her long fair hair, a beauty seen so rarely in Italy, that Raffaelle, believing it divine, has appropriated it to all his Madonnas, curtained a lovely forehead, and fell in flowing locks over her shoulders. Her azure eyes bore a heavenly expression; she was of middle height, exquisitely proportioned; and during the rare moments when a gleam of happiness allowed her natural character to display itself, she was lively, joyous, and sympathetic, but at the same time evinced a firm and decided disposition.

To make sure of her custody, Francesco kept her shut up in a remote apartment of his palace, the key of which he kept in his own possession. There, her unnatural and inflexible gaoler daily brought her some food. Up to the age of thirteen, which she had now reached, he had behaved to her with the most extreme harshness and severity; but now, to poor Beatrice's great astonishment, he all at once became gentle and even tender. Beatrice was a child no longer; her beauty expanded like a flower; and Francesco, a stranger to no crime, however heinous, had marked her for his own.

Brought up as she had been, uneducated, deprived of all society, even that of her stepmother, Beatrice knew not good from evil: her ruin was comparatively easy to compass; yet Francesco, to accomplish his diabolical purpose, employed all the means at his command. Every night she was awakened by a concert of music which seemed to come from Paradise. When she mentioned this to her father, he left her in this belief, adding that if she proved gentle and obedient she would be rewarded by heavenly sights, as well as heavenly sounds.

One night it came to pass that as the young girl was reposing, her head supported on her elbow, and listening to a delightful harmony, the chamber door suddenly opened, and from the darkness of her own room she beheld a suite of apartments brilliantly illuminated, and sensuous with perfumes; beautiful youths and girls, half clad, such as she had seen in the pictures of Guido and Raffaelle, moved to and fro in these apartments, seeming full of joy and happiness: these were the ministers to the pleasures of Francesco, who, rich as a king, every night revelled in the orgies of Alexander, the wedding revels of Lucrezia, and the excesses of Tiberius at Capri. After an hour, the door closed, and the seductive vision vanished, leaving Beatrice full of trouble and amazement.

The night following, the same apparition again presented itself, only, on this occasion, Francesco Cenci, undressed, entered his daughter's room and invited her to join the fete. Hardly knowing what she did, Beatrice yet perceived the impropriety of yielding to her father's wishes: she replied that, not seeing her stepmother, Lucrezia Petroni, among all these women, she dared not leave her bed to mix with persons who were unknown to her. Francesco threatened and prayed, but threats and prayers were of no avail. Beatrice wrapped herself up in the bedclothes, and obstinately refused to obey.

The next night she threw herself on her bed without undressing. At the accustomed hour the door opened, and the nocturnal spectacle reappeared. This time, Lucrezia Petroni was among the women who passed before Beatrice's door; violence had compelled her to undergo this humiliation. Beatrice was too far off to see her blushes and her tears. Francesco pointed out her stepmother, whom she had looked for in vain the previous evening; and as she could no longer make any opposition, he led her, covered with blushes and confusion, into the middle of this orgy.

Beatrice there saw incredible and infamous things...

Nevertheless, she resisted a long time: an inward voice

told her that this was horrible; but Francesco had the slow persistence of a demon. To these sights, calculated to stimulate her passions, he added heresies designed to warp her mind; he told her that the greatest saints venerated by the Church were the issue of fathers and daughters, and in the end Beatrice committed a crime without even knowing it to be a sin.

His brutality then knew no bounds. He forced Lucrezia and Beatrice to share the same bed, threatening his wife to kill her if she disclosed to his daughter by a single word that there was anything odious in such an intercourse. So matters went on for about three years.

At this time Francesco was obliged to make a journey, and leave the women alone and free. The first thing Lucrezia did was to enlighten Beatrice on the infamy of the life they were leading; they then together prepared a memorial to the pope, in which they laid before him a statement of all the blows and outrages they had suffered. But, before leaving, Francesco Cenci had taken precautions; every person about the pope was in his pay, or hoped to be. The petition never reached His Holiness, and the two poor women, remembering that Clement VIII had on a former occasion driven Giacomo, Cristaforo, and Rocco from his presence, thought they were included in the same proscription, and looked upon themselves as abandoned to their fate.

When matters were in this state, Giacomo, taking advantage of his father's absence, came to pay them a visit with a friend of his, an abbe named Guerra: he was a young man of twenty-five or twenty-six, belonging to one of the most noble families in Rome, of a bold, resolute, and courageous character, and idolised by all the Roman ladies for his beauty. To classical features he added blue eyes swimming in poetic sentiment; his hair was long and fair, with chestnut beard and eyebrows; add to these attractions a highly educated mind, natural eloquence expressed by a musical and penetrating voice, and the reader may form some idea of Monsignor the Abbe Guerra.

No sooner had he seen Beatrice than he fell in love with her. On her side, she was not slow to return the sympathy of the young priest. The Council of Trent had not been held at that time, consequently ecclesiastics were not precluded from marriage. It was therefore decided that on the return of Francesco the Abbe Guerra should demand the hand of Beatrice from her father, and the women, happy in the absence of their master, continued to live on, hoping for better things to come.

After three or four months, during which no one knew where he was, Francesco returned. The very first night, he wished to resume his intercourse with Beatrice; but she was no longer the same person, the timid and submissive child had become a girl of decided will; strong in her love for the abbe, she resisted alike prayers, threats, and blows.

The wrath of Francesco fell upon his wife, whom he accused of betraying him; he gave her a violent thrashing. Lucrezia Petroni was a veritable Roman she-wolf, passionate alike in love and vengeance; she endured all, but pardoned nothing.

Some days after this, the Abbe Guerra arrived at the Cenci palace to carry out what had been arranged. Rich, young, noble, and handsome, everything would seem to promise him success; yet he was rudely dismissed by Francesco. The first refusal did not daunt him; he returned to the charge a second time and yet a third, insisting upon the suitableness of such a union. At length Francesco, losing patience, told this obstinate lover that a reason existed why Beatrice could be neither his wife nor any other man's. Guerra demanded what this reason was. Francesco replied:

'Because she is my mistress.'

Monsignor Guerra turned pale at this answer, although at first he did not believe a word of it; but when he saw the smile with which Francesco Cenci accompanied his words, he was compelled to believe that, terrible though it was, the truth had been spoken.

For three days he sought an interview with Beatrice in vain; at length he succeeded in finding her. His last hope was her denial of this horrible story: Beatrice confessed all. Henceforth there was no human hope for the two lovers; an impassable gulf separated them. They parted bathed in tears, promising to love one another always.

Up to that time the two women had not formed any criminal resolution, and possibly the tragical incident might never have happened, had not Francesco one night returned into his daughter's room and violently forced her into the commission of fresh crime.

Henceforth the doom of Francesco was irrevocably pronounced.

As we have said, the mind of Beatrice was susceptible to the best and the worst influences: it could attain excellence, and descend to guilt. She went and told her mother of the fresh outrage she had undergone; this roused in the heart of the other woman the sting of her own wrongs; and, stimulating each other's desire for revenge, they decided upon the murder of Francesco.

Guerra was called in to this council of death. His heart was a prey to hatred and revenge. He undertook to communicate with Giacomo Cenci, without whose concurrence the women would not act, as he was the head of the family, when his father was left out of account.

Giacomo entered readily into the conspiracy. It will be remembered what he had formerly suffered from his father; since that time he had married, and the close-fisted old man had left him, with his wife and children, to languish in poverty. Guerra's house was selected to meet in and concert matters.

Giacomo hired a sbirro named Marzio, and Guerra a second named Olympio.

Both these men had private reasons for committing the crime—one being actuated by love, the other by hatred. Marzio, who was in the service of Giacomo, had often seen Beatrice, and loved her, but with that silent and hopeless love which devours the soul. When he conceived that the proposed crime would draw him nearer to Beatrice, he accepted his part in it without any demur.

As for Olympio, he hated Francesco, because the latter had caused him to lose the post of castellan of Rocco Petrella, a fortified stronghold in the kingdom of Naples, belonging to Prince Colonna. Almost every year Francesco Cenci spent some months at Rocco Petrella with his family; for Prince Colonna, a noble and magnificent but needy prince, had much esteem for Francesco, whose purse he found extremely useful. It had so happened that Francesco, being dissatisfied with Olympio, complained about him to Prince Colonna, and he was dismissed.

After several consultations between the Cenci family, the abbe and the sbirri, the following plan of action was decided upon.

The period when Francesco Cenci was accustomed to go to Rocco Petrella was approaching: it was arranged that Olympio, conversant with the district and its inhabitants, should collect a party of a dozen Neapolitan bandits, and conceal them in a forest through which the travellers would have to pass. Upon a given signal, the whole family were to be seized and carried off. A heavy ransom was to be demanded, and the sons were to be sent back to Rome to raise the sum; but, under pretext of inability to do so, they were to allow the time fixed by the bandits to lapse, when Francesco was to be put to death. Thus all suspicions of a plot would be avoided, and the real assassins would escape justice.

This well-devised scheme was nevertheless unsuccessful. When Francesco left Rome, the scout sent in advance by the conspirators could not find the bandits; the latter, not being warned beforehand, failed to come down before the passage of the travellers, who arrived safe and sound at Rocco Petrella. The bandits, after having patrolled the road in vain, came to the conclusion that their prey had escaped, and, unwilling to stay any longer in a place where they had already spent a week, went off in quest of better luck elsewhere.

Francesco had in the meantime settled down in the fortress, and, to be more free to tyrannise over Lucrezia and Beatrice, sent back to Rome Giacomo and his two other sons. He then recommenced his infamous attempts upon Beatrice, and with such persistence, that she resolved herself to accomplish the deed which at first she desired to entrust to other hands.

Olympio and Marzio, who had nothing to fear from justice, remained lurking about the castle; one day Beatrice saw them from a window, and made signs that she had something to communicate to them. The same night Olympio, who having been castellan knew all the approaches to the fortress, made his way there with his companion. Beatrice awaited them at a window which looked on to a secluded courtyard; she gave them letters which she had written to her brother and to Monsignor Guerra. The former was to approve, as he had done before, the murder of their father; for she would do nothing without his sanction. As for Monsignor Guerra, he was to pay Olympio a thousand piastres, half the stipulated sum; Marzio acting out of pure love for Beatrice, whom he worshipped as a Madonna; which observing, the girl gave him a handsome scarlet mantle, trimmed with gold lace, telling him to wear it for love of her. As for the remaining moiety, it was to be paid when the death of the old man had placed his wife and daughter in possession of his fortune.

The two sbirri departed, and the imprisoned conspirators anxiously awaited their return. On the day fixed, they were seen again. Monsignor Guerra had paid the thousand piastres, and Giacomo had given his consent. Nothing now stood in the way of the execution of this terrible deed, which was fixed for the 8th of September, the day of the Nativity of the Virgin; but Signora Lucrezia, a very devout person, having noticed this circumstance, would not be a party to the committal of a double sin; the matter was therefore deferred till the next day, the 9th.

That evening, the 9th of September, 1598, the two women, supping with the old man, mixed some narcotic with his wine so adroitly that, suspicious though he was, he never detected it, and having swallowed the potion, soon fell into a deep sleep.

The evening previous, Marzio and Olympio had been admitted into the castle, where they had lain concealed all night and all day; for, as will be remembered, the assassination would have been effected the day before had it not been for the religious scruples of Signora Lucrezia Petroni. Towards midnight, Beatrice fetched them out of their hiding-place, and took them to her father's chamber, the door of which she herself opened. The assassins entered, and the two women awaited the issue in the room adjoining.

After a moment, seeing the sbirri reappear pale and nerveless, shaking their heads without speaking, they at once inferred that nothing had been done.

'What is the matter?' cried Beatrice; 'and what hinders you?'

'It is a cowardly act,' replied the assassins, 'to kill a poor old man in his sleep. At the thought of his age, we were struck with pity.'

Then Beatrice disdainfully raised her head, and in a deep firm voice thus reproached them:—

'Is it possible that you, who pretend to be brave and strong, have not courage enough to kill a sleeping old man? How would it be if he were awake? And thus you steal our money! Very well: since your cowardice compels me to do so, I will kill my father myself; but you will not long survive him.'

Hearing these words, the sbirri felt ashamed of their irresolution, and, indicating by signs that they would fulfil their compact, they entered the room, accompanied by the two women. As they had said, a ray of moonlight shone through the open window, and brought into prominence the tranquil face of the old man, the sight of whose white hair had so affected them.

This time they showed no mercy. One of them carried two great nails, such as those portrayed in pictures of the Crucifixion; the other bore a mallet: the first placed a nail upright over one of the old man's eyes; the other struck it with the hammer, and drove it into his head. The throat was pierced in the same way with the second nail; and thus the guilty soul, stained throughout its career with crimes of violence, was in its turn violently torn from the body, which lay writhing on the floor where it had rolled.

The young girl then, faithful to her word, handed the sbirri a large purse containing the rest of the sum agreed upon, and they left. When they found themselves alone, the women drew the nails out of the wounds, wrapped the corpse in a sheet, and dragged it through the rooms towards a small rampart, intending to throw it down into a garden which had been allowed to run to waste. They hoped that the old man's death would be attributed to his having accidentally fallen off the terrace on his way in the dark to a closet at the end of the gallery. But their strength failed them when they reached the door of the last room, and, while resting there, Lucrezia perceived the two sbirri, sharing the money before making their escape. At her call they came to her, carried the corpse to the rampart, and, from a spot pointed out by the women, where the terrace was unfenced by any parapet, they threw it into an elder tree below, whose branches retained it suspended.

When the body was found the following morning hanging in the branches of the elder tree, everybody supposed, as Beatrice and her stepmother had foreseen, that Francesco, stepping over the edge of the 386 terrace in the dark, had thus met his end. The body was so scratched and disfigured that no one noticed the wounds made by the two nails. The ladies, as soon as the news was imparted to them, came out from their rooms, weeping and lamenting in so natural a manner as to disarm any suspicions. The only person who formed any was the laundress to whom Beatrice entrusted the sheet in which her father's body had been wrapped, accounting for its bloody condition by a lame explanation, which the laundress accepted without question, or pretended to do so; and immediately after the funeral, the mourners returned to Rome, hoping at length to enjoy quietude and peace. For some time, indeed, they did enjoy tranquillity, perhaps poisoned by remorse, but ere long retribution pursued them. The court of Naples, hearing of the sudden and unexpected death of Francesco Cenci, and conceiving some suspicions of violence, despatched a royal commissioner to Petrella to exhume the body and make minute inquiries, if there appeared to be adequate grounds for doing so. On his arrival all the domestics in the castle were placed under arrest and sent in chains to Naples. No incriminating proofs, however, were found, except in the evidence of the laundress, who deposed that Beatrice had given her a bloodstained sheet to wash. This clue led to terrible consequences; for, further questioned, she declared that she could not believe the explanation given to account for its condition. The evidence was sent to the Roman court; but at that period it did not appear strong enough to warrant the arrest of the Cenci family, who remained undisturbed for many months, during which time the youngest boy died. Of the five brothers there only remained Giacomo, the eldest, and Bernardo, the youngest but one. Nothing prevented them from escaping to Venice or Florence; but they remained quietly in Rome.

Meantime Monsignor Guerra received private information that, shortly before the death of Francesco, Marzio and Olympio had been seen prowling round the castle, and that the Neapolitan police had received orders to arrest them.

The monsignor was a most wary man, and very difficult to catch napping when warned in time. He immediately hired two other sbirri to assassinate Marzio and Olympio. The one commissioned to put Olympio out of the way came across him at Terni, and conscientiously did his work with a poniard, but Marzio's man unfortunately arrived at Naples too late, and found his bird already in the hands of the police.

He was put to the torture, and confessed everything. His deposition was sent to Rome, whither he shortly afterwards followed it, to be confronted with the accused. Warrants were immediately issued for the arrest of Giacomo, Bernardo, Lucrezia, and Beatrice; they were at first confined in the Cenci palace under a strong guard, but the proofs against them becoming stronger and stronger, they were removed to the castle of Corte Savella, where they were confronted with Marzio; but they obstinately denied both any complicity in the crime and any knowledge of the assassin. Beatrice, above all, displayed the greatest assurance, demanding to be the first to be confronted with Marzio; whose mendacity she affirmed with such calm dignity, that he, more than ever smitten by her beauty, determined, since he could not live for her, to save her by his death. Consequently, he declared all his statements to be false, and asked forgiveness from God and from Beatrice; neither threats nor tortures could make him recant, and he died firm in his denial, under frightful tortures. The Cenci then thought themselves safe.

God's justice, however, still pursued them. The sbirro who had killed Olympio happened to be arrested for another crime, and, making a clean breast, confessed that he had been employed by Monsignor Guerra—to put out of the way a fellow-assassin named Olympio, who knew too many of the monsignor's secrets.

Luckily for himself, Monsignor Guerra heard of this opportunely. A man of infinite resource, he lost not a moment in timid or irresolute plans, but as it happened that at the very moment when he was warned, the charcoal dealer who supplied his house with fuel was at hand, he sent for him, purchased his silence with a handsome bribe, and then, buying for almost their weight in gold the dirty old clothes which he wore, he assumed these, cut off all his beautiful cherished fair hair, stained his beard, smudged his face, bought two asses, laden with charcoal, and limped up and down the streets of Rome, crying, 'Charcoal! charcoal!' Then, whilst all the detectives were hunting high and low for him, he got out of the city, met a company of merchants under escort, joined them, and reached Naples, where he embarked. What ultimately became of him was never known; it has been asserted, but without confirmation, that he succeeded in reaching France, and enlisted in a Swiss regiment in the pay of Henry IV.

The confession of the sbirro and the disappearance of Monsignor Guerra left no moral doubt of the guilt of the Cenci. They were consequently sent from the castle to the prison; the two brothers, when put to the torture, broke down and confessed their guilt. Lucrezia Petroni's full habit of body rendered her unable to bear the torture of the rope, and, on being suspended in the air, begged to be lowered, when she confessed all she knew.

As for Beatrice, she continued unmoved; neither promises, threats, nor torture had any effect upon her; she bore everything unflinchingly, and the judge Ulysses Moscati himself, famous though he was in such matters, failed to draw from her a single incriminating word. Unwilling to take any further responsibility, he referred the case to Clement VIII; and the pope, conjecturing that the judge had been too lenient in applying the torture to a young and beautiful Roman lady, took it out of his hands and entrusted it to another judge, whose severity and insensibility to emotion were undisputed.

This latter reopened the whole interrogatory, and as Beatrice up to that time had only been subjected to the ordinary torture, he gave instructions to apply both the ordinary and extraordinary. This was the rope and pulley, one of the most terrible inventions ever devised by the most ingenious of tormentors.

To make the nature of this horrid torture plain to our readers, we give a detailed description of it, adding an extract of the presiding judge's report of the case, taken from the Vatican manuscripts.

Of the various forms of torture then used in Rome the most common were the whistle, the fire, the sleepless, and the rope.

The mildest, the torture of the whistle, was used only in the case of children and old persons; it consisted in thrusting between the nails and the flesh reeds cut in the shape of whistles.

The fire, frequently employed before the invention of the sleepless torture, was simply roasting the soles of the feet before a hot fire.

The sleepless torture, invented by Marsilius, was worked by forcing the accused into an angular frame of wood about five feet high, the sufferer being stripped and his arms tied behind his back to the frame; two men, relieved every five swung about by the executioner, either like the pendulum of a clock, or by elevating him with the windlass and dropping him to within a foot or two of the ground. If he stood this torture, a thing almost unheard of, seeing that it cut the flesh of the wrist to the bone and dislocated the limbs, weights were attached to the feet, thus doubling the torture. This last form of torture was only applied when an atrocious crime had been proved to have been committed upon a sacred person, such as a priest, a cardinal, a prince, or an eminent and learned man.

Having seen that Beatrice was sentenced to the torture ordinary and extraordinary, and having explained the nature of these tortures, we proceed to quote the official report:—

'And as in reply to every question she would confess nothing, we caused her to be taken by two officers and led from the prison to the torture chamber, where the torturer was in attendance; there, after cutting off her hair, he made her sit on a small stool, undressed her, pulled off her shoes, tied her hands behind her back, fastened them to a rope passed over a pulley bolted into the ceiling of the aforesaid chamber, and wound up at the other end by a four lever windlass, worked by two men.

'Before hoisting her from the ground we again interrogated her touching the aforesaid parricide; but notwithstanding the confessions of her brother and her stepmother, which were again produced, bearing their signatures, she persisted in denying everything, saying, "Haul me about and do what you like with me; I have spoken the truth, and will tell you nothing else, even if I were torn to pieces."

'Upon this we had her hoisted in the air by the wrists to the height of about two feet from the ground, while we recited a Pater Noster; and then again questioned her as to the facts and circumstances of the aforesaid parricide; but she would make no further answer, only saying, "You are killing me! You are killing me!"

hours, sat beside him, and roused him the moment he closed his eyes. Marsilius says he has never found a man proof against this torture; but here he claims more than he is justly entitled to. Farinacci states that, out of one hundred accused persons subjected to it, five only refused to confess—a very satisfactory result for the inventor.

Lastly comes the torture of the rope and pulley, the most in vogue of all, and known in other Latin countries as the strappado.

It was divided into three degrees of intensity—the slight, the severe, and the very severe.

The first, or slight torture, which consisted mainly in the apprehensions it caused, comprised the threat of severe torture, introduction into the torture chamber, stripping, and the tying of the rope in readiness for its appliance. To increase the terror these preliminaries excited, a pang of physical pain was added by tightening a cord round the wrists. This often sufficed to extract a confession from women or men of highly strung nerves.

The second degree, or severe torture, consisted in fastening the sufferer, stripped naked, and his hands tied behind his back, by the wrists to one end of a rope passed round a pulley bolted into the vaulted ceiling, the other end being attached to a windlass, by turning which he could be hoisted into the air, and dropped again, either slowly or with a jerk, as ordered by the judge. The suspension generally lasted during the recital of a Pater Noster, an Ave Maria, or a Miserere; if the accused persisted in his denial, it was doubled. This second degree, the last of the ordinary torture, was put in practice when the crime appeared reasonably probable but was not absolutely proved.

The third, or very severe, the first of the extraordinary forms of torture, was so called when the sufferer, having hung suspended by the wrists, for sometimes a whole hour, was

'We then raised her to the elevation of four feet, and began an Ave Maria. But before our prayer was half finished she fainted away; or pretended to do so.

'We caused a bucketful of water to be thrown over her head; feeling its coolness, she recovered consciousness, and cried, "My God! I am dead! You are killing me! My God!" But this was all she would say.

'We then raised her higher still, and recited a Miserere, during which, instead of joining in the prayer, she shook convulsively and cried several times, "My God! My God!"

'Again questioned as to the aforesaid parricide, she would confess nothing, saying only that she was innocent, and then again fainted away.

'We caused more water to be thrown over her; then she recovered her senses, opened her eyes, and cried, "O cursed executioners! You are killing me! You are killing me!" But nothing more would she say.

'Seeing which, and that she persisted in her denial, we ordered the torturer to proceed to the torture by jerks.

'He accordingly hoisted her ten feet from the ground, and when there we enjoined her to tell the truth; but whether she would not or could not speak, she answered only by a motion of the head indicating that she could say nothing.

'Seeing which, we made a sign to the executioner, to let go the rope, and she fell with all her weight from the height of ten feet to that of two feet; her arms, from the shock, were dislocated from their sockets; she uttered a loud cry, and swooned away.

'We again caused water to be dashed in her face; she returned to herself, and again cried out, "Infamous assassins! You are killing me; but were you to tear out my arms, I would tell you nothing else."

'Upon this, we ordered a weight of fifty pounds to be

fastened to her feet. But at this moment the door opened, and many voices cried, "Enough! Enough! Do not torture her any more!"'

These voices were those of Giacomo, Bernardo, and Lucrezia Petroni. The judges, perceiving the obstinacy of Beatrice, had ordered that the accused, who had been separated for five months, should be confronted.

They advanced into the torture chamber, and seeing Beatrice hanging by the wrists, her arms disjointed, and covered with blood, Giacomo cried out:—

'The sin is committed; nothing further remains but to save our souls by repentance, undergo death courageously, and not suffer you to be thus tortured.'

Then said Beatrice, shaking her head as if to cast off grief—

'Do you then wish to die? Since you wish it, be it so.'

Then turning to the officers:—

'Untie me,' said she, 'read the examination to me; and what I have to confess, I will confess; what I have to deny, I will deny.'

Beatrice was then lowered and untied; a barber reduced the dislocation of her arms in the usual manner; the examination was read over to her, and, as she had promised, she made a full confession.

After this confession, at the request of the two brothers, they were all confined in the same prison; but the next day Giacomo and Bernardo were taken to the cells of Tordinona; as for the women, they remained where they were.

The pope was so horrified on reading the particulars of the crime contained in the confessions, that he ordered the culprits to be dragged by wild horses through the streets of Rome. But so barbarous a sentence shocked the public mind, so much so that many persons of princely rank petitioned the Holy Father on their knees, imploring him to reconsider his decree, or at least allow the accused to be heard in their defence.

'Tell me,' replied Clement VIII, 'did they give their unhappy father time to be heard in his own defence, when they slew him in so merciless and degrading a fashion?'

At length, overcome by so many entreaties, he respited them for three days.

The most eloquent and skilful advocates in Rome immediately busied themselves in preparing pleadings for so emotional a case, and on the day fixed for hearing appeared before His Holiness.

The first pleader was Nicolo degli Angeli, who spoke with such force and eloquence that the pope, alarmed at the effect he was producing among the audience, passionately interrupted him.

'Are there then to be found,' he indignantly cried, 'among the Roman nobility children capable of killing their parents, and among Roman lawyers men capable of speaking in their defence? This is a thing we should never have believed, nor even for a moment supposed it possible!'

All were silent upon this terrible rebuke, except Farinacci, who, nerving himself with a strong sense of duty, replied respectfully but firmly—

'Most Holy Father, we are not here to defend criminals, but to save the innocent; for if we succeeded in proving that any of the accused acted in self-defence, I hope that they will be exonerated in the eyes of your Holiness; for just as the law provides for cases in which the father may legally kill the child, so this holds good in the converse. We will therefore continue our pleadings on receiving leave from your Holiness to do so.'

Clement VIII then showed himself as patient as he had previously been hasty, and heard the argument of Farinacci, who pleaded that Francesco Cenci had lost all the rights of a father from the day that he violated his daughter. In support of his contention he wished to put in the memorial sent by

Beatrice to His Holiness, petitioning him, as her sister had done, to remove her from the paternal roof and place her in a convent. Unfortunately, this petition had disappeared, and notwithstanding the minutest search among the papal documents, no trace of it could be found.

The pope had all the pleadings collected, and dismissed the advocates, who then retired, excepting d'Altieri, who knelt before him, saying—

'Most Holy Father, I humbly ask pardon for appearing before you in this case, but I had no choice in the matter, being the advocate of the poor.'

The pope kindly raised him, saying:

'Go; we are not surprised at your conduct, but at that of others, who protect and defend criminals.'

As the pope took a great interest in this case, he sat up all night over it, studying it with Cardinal di San Marcello, a man of much acumen and great experience in criminal cases. Then, having summed it up, he sent a draft of his opinion to the advocates, who read it with great satisfaction, and entertained hopes that the lives of the convicted persons would be spared; for the evidence all went to prove that even if the children had taken their father's life, all the provocation came from him, and that Beatrice in particular had been dragged into the part she had taken in this crime by the tyranny, wickedness, and brutality of her father. Under the influence of these considerations the pope mitigated the severity of their prison life, and even allowed the prisoners to hope that their lives would not be forfeited.

Amidst the general feeling of relief afforded to the public by these favours, another tragical event changed the papal mind and frustrated all his humane intentions. This was the atrocious murder of the Marchese di Santa Croce, a man seventy years of age, by his son Paolo, who stabbed him with a dagger in fifteen or twenty places, because the father would not promise to make Paolo his sole heir. The murderer fled and escaped.

Clement VIII was horror-stricken at the increasing frequency of this crime of parricide: for the moment, however, he was unable to take action, having to go to Monte Cavallo to consecrate a cardinal titular bishop in the church of Santa Maria degli Angeli; but the day following, on Friday the 10th of September 1599, at eight o'clock in the morning, he summoned Monsignor Taverna, governor of Rome, and said to him—

'Monsignor, we place in your hands the Cenci case, that you may carry out the sentence as speedily as possible.'

On his return to his palace, after leaving His Holiness, the governor convened a meeting of all the criminal judges in the city, the result of the council being that all the Cenci were condemned to death.

The final sentence was immediately known; and as this unhappy family inspired a constantly increasing interest, many cardinals spent the whole of the night either on horseback or in their carriages, making interest that, at least so far as the women were concerned, they should be put to death privately and in the prison, and that a free pardon should be granted to Bernardo, a poor lad only fifteen years of age, who, guiltless of any participation in the crime, yet found himself involved in its consequences. The one who interested himself most in the case was Cardinal Sforza, who nevertheless failed to elicit a single gleam of hope, so obdurate was His Holiness. At length Farinacci, working on the papal conscience, succeeded, after long and urgent entreaties, and only at the last moment, that the life of Bernardo should be spared.

From Friday evening the members of the brotherhood of the Conforteria had gathered at the two prisons of Corte Savella and Tordinona. The preparations for the closing scene of the tragedy had occupied workmen on the bridge of Sant' Angelo all night; and it was not till five o'clock in the morning that the registrar entered the cell of Lucrezia and Beatrice to read their sentences to them.

Both were sleeping, calm in the belief of a reprieve. The registrar woke them, and told them that, judged by man, they must now prepare to appear before God.

Beatrice was at first thunderstruck: she seemed paralysed and speechless; then she rose from bed, and staggering as if intoxicated, recovered her speech, uttering despairing cries. Lucrezia heard the tidings with more firmness, and proceeded to dress herself to go to the chapel, exhorting Beatrice to resignation; but she, raving, wrung her hands and struck her head against the wall, shrieking, 'To die! to die! Am I to die unprepared, on a scaffold! on a gibbet! My God! my God!' This fit led to a terrible paroxysm, after which the exhaustion of her body enabled her mind to recover its balance, and from that moment she became an angel of humility and an example of resignation.

Her first request was for a notary to make her will. This was immediately complied with, and on his arrival she dictated its provisions with much calmness and precision. Its last clause desired her interment in the church of San Pietro in Montorio, for which she always had a strong attachment, as it commanded a view of her father's palace. She bequeathed five hundred crowns to the nuns of the order of the Stigmata, and ordered that her dowry, amounting to fifteen thousand crowns, should be distributed in marriage portions to fifty poor girls. She selected the foot of the high altar as the place where she wished to be buried, over which hung the beautiful picture of the Transfiguration, so often admired by her during her life.

Following her example, Lucrezia in her turn, disposed of her property: she desired to be buried in the church of San Giorgio di Velobre, and left thirty-two thousand crowns to charities, with other pious legacies. Having settled their earthly affairs, they joined in prayer, reciting psalms, litanies, and prayers for the dying.

At eight o'clock they confessed, heard mass, and received the sacraments; after which Beatrice, observing to her stepmother that the rich dresses they wore were out of place on a scaffold, ordered two to be made in nun's fashion—that is to say, gathered at the neck, with long wide sleeves. That for Lucrezia was made of black cotton stuff, Beatrice's of taffetas. In addition she had a small black turban made to place on her head. These dresses, with cords for girdles, were brought them; they were placed on a chair, while the women continued to pray.

The time appointed being near at hand, they were informed that their last moment was approaching. Then Beatrice, who was still on her knees, rose with a tranquil and almost joyful countenance. 'Mother,' said she, 'the moment of our suffering is impending; I think we had better dress in these clothes, and help one another at our toilet for the last time.' They then put on the dresses provided, girt themselves with the cords; Beatrice placed her turban on her head, and they awaited the last summons.

In the meantime, Giacomo and Bernardo, whose sentences had been read to them, awaited also the moment of their death. About ten o'clock the members of the Confraternity of Mercy, a Florentine order, arrived at the prison of Tordinona, and halted on the threshold with the crucifix, awaiting the appearance of the unhappy youths. Here a serious accident had nearly happened. As many persons were at the prison windows to see the prisoners come out, someone accidentally threw down a large flower-pot full of earth, which fell into the street and narrowly missed one of the Confraternity who was amongst the torch-bearers just before the crucifix. It passed so close to the torch as to extinguish the flame in its descent.

At this moment the gates opened, and Giacomo appeared

first on the threshold. He fell on his knees, adoring the holy crucifix with great devotion. He was completely covered with a large mourning cloak, under which his bare breast was prepared to be torn by the red-hot pincers of the executioner, which were lying ready in a chafing-dish fixed to the cart. Having ascended the vehicle, in which the executioner placed him so as more readily to perform this office, Bernardo came out, and was thus addressed on his appearance by the fiscal of Rome—

'Signor Bernardo Cenci, in the name of our blessed Redeemer, our Holy Father the Pope spares your life; with the sole condition that you accompany your relatives to the scaffold and to their death, and never forget to pray for those with whom you were condemned to die.'

At this unexpected intelligence, a loud murmur of joy spread among the crowd, and the members of the Confraternity immediately untied the small mask which covered the youth's eyes; for, owing to his tender age, it had been thought proper to conceal the scaffold from his sight.

Then the executioner; having disposed of Giacomo, came down from the cart to take Bernardo; whose pardon being formally communicated to him, he took off his handcuffs, and placed him alongside his brother, covering him up with a magnificent cloak embroidered with gold, for the neck and shoulders of the poor lad had been already bared, as a preliminary to his decapitation. People were surprised to see such a rich cloak in the possession of the executioner, but were told that it was the one given by Beatrice to Marzio to pledge him to the murder of her father, which fell to the executioner as a perquisite after the execution of the assassin. The sight of the great assemblage of people produced such an effect upon the boy that he fainted.

The procession then proceeded to the prison of Corte Savella, marching to the sound of funeral chants. At its gates the sacred crucifix halted for the women to join: they soon appeared, fell on their knees, and worshipped the holy symbol as the others had done. The march to the scaffold was then resumed.

The two female prisoners followed the last row of penitents in single file, veiled to the waist, with the distinction that Lucrezia, as a widow, wore a black veil and high-heeled slippers of the same hue, with bows of ribbon, as was the fashion; whilst Beatrice, as a young unmarried girl, wore a silk flat cap to match her corsage, with a plush hood, which fell over her shoulders and covered her violet frock; white slippers with high heels, ornamented with gold rosettes and cherry-coloured fringe. The arms of both were untrammelled, except for a thin slack cord which left their hands free to carry a crucifix and a handkerchief.

During the night a lofty scaffold had been erected on the bridge of Sant' Angelo, and the plank and block were placed thereon. Above the block was hung, from a large cross beam, a ponderous axe, which, guided by two grooves, fell with its whole weight at the touch of a spring.

In this formation the procession wended its way towards the bridge of Sant' Angelo. Lucrezia, the more broken down of the two, wept bitterly; but Beatrice was firm and unmoved. On arriving at the open space before the bridge, the women were led into a chapel, where they were shortly joined by Giacomo and Bernardo; they remained together for a few moments, when the brothers were led away to the scaffold, although one was to be executed last, and the other was pardoned. But when they had mounted the platform, Bernardo fainted a second time; and as the executioner was approaching to his assistance, some of the crowd, supposing that his object was to decapitate him, cried loudly, 'He is pardoned!' The executioner reassured them by seating Bernardo near the block, Giacomo kneeling on the other side.

Then the executioner descended, entered the chapel, and reappeared leading Lucrezia, who was the first to suffer. At the foot of the scaffold he tied her hands behind her back, tore open the top of her corsage so as to uncover her shoulders, gave her the crucifix to kiss, and led her to the step ladder, which she ascended with great difficulty, on account of her extreme stoutness; then, on her reaching the platform, he removed the veil which covered her head. On this exposure of her features to the immense crowd, Lucrezia shuddered from head to foot; then, her eyes full of tears, she cried with a loud voice—

'O my God, have mercy upon me; and do you, brethren, pray for my soul!'

Having uttered these words, not knowing what was required of her, she turned to Alessandro, the chief executioner, and asked what she was to do; he told her to bestride the plank and lie prone upon it; which she did with great trouble and timidity; but as she was unable, on account of the fullness of her bust, to lay her neck upon the block, this had to be raised by placing a billet of wood underneath it; all this time the poor woman, suffering even more from shame than from fear, was kept in suspense; at length, when she was properly adjusted, the executioner touched the spring, the knife fell, and the decapitated head, falling on the platform of the scaffold, bounded two or three times in the air, to the general horror; the executioner then seized it, showed it to the multitude, and wrapping it in black taffetas, placed it with the body on a bier at the foot of the scaffold.

Whilst arrangements were being made for the decapitation of Beatrice, several stands, full of spectators, broke down; some people were killed by this accident, and still more lamed and injured.

The machine being now rearranged and washed, the

executioner returned to the chapel to take charge of Beatrice, who, on seeing the sacred crucifix, said some prayers for her soul, and on her hands being tied, cried out, 'God grant that you be binding this body unto corruption, and loosing this soul unto life eternal!' She then arose, proceeded to the platform, where she devoutly kissed the stigmata; then, leaving her slippers at the foot of the scaffold, she nimbly ascended the ladder, and instructed beforehand, promptly lay down on the plank, without exposing her naked shoulders. But her precautions to shorten the bitterness of death were of no avail, for the pope, knowing her impetuous disposition, and fearing lest she might be led into the commission of some sin between absolution and death, had given orders that the moment Beatrice was extended on the scaffold a signal gun should be fired from the castle of Sant' Angelo; which was done, to the great astonishment of everybody, including Beatrice herself, who, not expecting this explosion, raised herself almost upright; the pope meanwhile, who was praying at Monte Cavallo, gave her absolution 'in articulo mortis'. About five minutes thus passed, during which the sufferer waited with her head replaced on the block; at length, when the executioner judged that the absolution had been given, he released the spring, and the axe fell.

A gruesome sight was then afforded: whilst the head bounced away on one side of the block, on the other the body rose erect, as if about to step backwards; the executioner exhibited the head, and disposed of it and the body as before. He wished to place Beatrice's body with that of her stepmother, but the brotherhood of Mercy took it out of his hands, and as one of them was attempting to lay it on the bier, it slipped from him and fell from the scaffold to the ground below; the dress being partially torn from the body, which was so besmeared with dust and blood that much time was occupied in washing it. Poor Bernardo was so overcome by this horrible scene that he swooned away for the third time, and it was necessary to revive him with stimulants to witness the fate of his elder brother.

The turn of Giacomo at length arrived: he had witnessed the death of his stepmother and his sister, and his clothes were covered with their blood; the executioner approached him and tore off his cloak, exposing his bare breast covered with the wounds caused by the grip of red-hot pincers; in this state, and half-naked, he rose to his feet, and turning to his brother, said—

'Bernardo, if in my examination I have compromised and accused you, I have done so falsely, and although I have already disavowed this declaration, I repeat, at the moment of appearing before God, that you are innocent, and that it is a cruel abuse of justice to compel you to witness this frightful spectacle.'

The executioner then made him kneel down, bound his legs to one of the beams erected on the scaffold, and having bandaged his eyes, shattered his head with a blow of his mallet; then, in the sight of all, he hacked his body into four quarters. The official party then left, taking with them Bernardo, who, being in a state of high fever, was bled and put to bed.

The corpses of the two ladies were laid out each on its bier under the statue of St. Paul, at the foot of the bridge, with four torches of white wax, which burned till four o'clock in the afternoon; then, along with the remains of Giacomo, they were taken to the church of San Giovanni Decollato; finally, about nine in the evening, the body of Beatrice, covered with flowers, and attired in the dress worn at her execution, was carried to the church of San Pietro in Montorio, with fifty lighted torches, and followed by the brethren of the order of the Stigmata and all the Franciscan monks in Rome; there, agreeably to her wish, it was buried at the foot of the high altar.

The same evening Signora Lucrezia was interred, as she had desired to be, in the church of San Giorgio di Velobre.

All Rome may be said to have been present at this tragedy,

carriages, horses, foot people, and cars crowding as it were upon one another. The day was unfortunately so hot, and the sun so scorching, that many persons fainted, others returned home stricken with fever, and some even died during the night, owing to sunstroke from exposure during the three hours occupied by the execution.

The Tuesday following, the 14th of September, being the Feast of the Holy Cross, the brotherhood of San Marcello, by special licence of the pope, set at liberty the unhappy Bernardo Cenci, with the condition of paying within the year two thousand five hundred Roman crowns to the brotherhood of the most Holy Trinity of Pope Sixtus, as may be found to-day recorded in their archives.

Having now seen the tomb, if you desire to form a more vivid impression of the principal actors in this tragedy than can be derived from a narrative, pay a visit to the Barberini Gallery, where you will see, with five other masterpieces by Guido, the portrait of Beatrice, taken, some say the night before her execution, others during her progress to the scaffold; it is the head of a lovely girl, wearing a headdress composed of a turban with a lappet. The hair is of a rich fair chestnut hue; the dark eyes are moistened with recent tears; a perfectly formed nose surmounts an infantile mouth; unfortunately, the loss of tone in the picture since it was painted has destroyed the original fair complexion. The age of the subject may be twenty, or perhaps twenty-two years.

Near this portrait is that of Lucrezia Petrani: the small head indicates a person below the middle height; the attributes are those of a Roman matron in her pride; her high complexion, graceful contour, straight nose, black eyebrows, and expression at the same time imperious and voluptuous indicate this character to the life; a smile still seems to linger on the charming dimpled cheeks and perfect mouth mentioned by the chronicler, and her face is exquisitely framed by luxuriant curls falling from her forehead in graceful profusion.

As for Giacomo and Bernardo, as no portraits of them are in existence, we are obliged to gather an idea of their appearance from the manuscript which has enabled us to compile this sanguinary history; they are thus described by the eye-witness of the closing scene—

Giacomo was short, well-made and strong, with black hair and beard; he appeared to be about twenty-six years of age.

Poor Bernardo was the image of his sister, so nearly resembling her, that when he mounted the scaffold his long hair and girlish face led people to suppose him to be Beatrice herself: he might be fourteen or fifteen years of age.

The peace of God be with them!

4

THE COUNTESS DE SAINT-GERAN

About the end of the year 1639, a troop of horsemen arrived, towards midday, in a little village at the northern extremity of the province of Auvergne, from the direction of Paris. The country folk assembled at the noise, and found it to proceed from the provost of the mounted police and his men. The heat was excessive, the horses were bathed in sweat, the horsemen covered with dust, and the party seemed on its return from an important expedition. A man left the escort, and asked an old woman who was spinning at her door if there was not an inn in the place. The woman and her children showed him a bush hanging over a door at the end of the only street in the village, and the escort recommenced its march at a walk. There was noticed, among the mounted men, a young man of distinguished appearance and richly dressed, who appeared to be a prisoner. This discovery redoubled the curiosity of the villagers, who followed the cavalcade as far as the door of the wine-shop. The host came out, cap in hand, and the provost enquired of him with a swaggering air if his pothouse was large enough to accommodate his troop, men and horses. The host replied that he had the best wine in the country to give to the king's servants, and that it would be easy to collect in the neighbourhood litter and forage enough for their horses. The provost listened contemptuously to these fine promises, gave the necessary orders as to what was to be done, and slid off his horse, uttering an oath proceeding from heat and fatigue. The horsemen clustered round the young man: one held his stirrup, and the provost deferentially gave way to him to enter the inn first. No more doubt could be entertained that he was a prisoner of importance, and all kinds of conjectures were made. The men maintained that he must be charged with a great crime, otherwise a young nobleman of his rank would never have been arrested; the women argued, on the contrary, that it was impossible for such a pretty youth not to be innocent.

Inside the inn all was bustle: the serving-lads ran from cellar to garret; the host swore and despatched his servant-girls to the neighbours, and the hostess scolded her daughter, flattening her nose against the panes of a downstairs window to admire the handsome youth.

There were two tables in the principal eating-room. The provost took possession of one, leaving the other to the soldiers, who went in turn to tether their horses under a shed in the back yard; then he pointed to a stool for the prisoner, and seated himself opposite to him, rapping the table with his thick cane.

'Ouf!' he cried, with a fresh groan of weariness, 'I heartily beg your pardon, marquis, for the bad wine I am giving you!'

The young man smiled gaily.

'The wine is all very well, monsieur provost,' said he, 'but I cannot conceal from you that however agreeable your company is to me, this halt is very inconvenient; I am in a hurry to get through my ridiculous situation, and I should have liked to arrive in time to stop this affair at once.'

The girl of the house was standing before the table with a pewter pot which she had just brought, and at these words she raised her eyes on the prisoner, with a reassured look which seemed to say, 'I was sure that he was innocent.'

'But,' continued the marquis, carrying the glass to his lips, 'this wine is not so bad as you say, monsieur provost.'

Then turning to the girl, who was eyeing his gloves and his ruff—

'To your health, pretty child.'

'Then,' said the provost, amazed at this free and easy air, 'perhaps I shall have to beg you to excuse your sleeping quarters.'

'What!' exclaimed the marquis, 'do we sleep here?'

'My lord;' said the provost, 'we have sixteen long leagues to make, our horses are done up, and so far as I am concerned I declare that I am no better than my horse.'

The marquis knocked on the table, and gave every indication of being greatly annoyed. The provost meanwhile puffed and blowed, stretched out his big boots, and mopped his forehead with his handkerchief. He was a portly man, with a puffy face, whom fatigue rendered singularly uncomfortable.

'Marquis,' said he, 'although your company, which affords me the opportunity of showing you some attention, is very precious to me, you cannot doubt that I had much rather enjoy it on another footing. If it be within your power, as you say, to release yourself from the hands of justice, the sooner you do so the better I shall be pleased. But I beg you to consider the state we are in. For my part, I am unfit to keep the saddle another hour, and are you not yourself knocked up by this forced march in the great heat?'

'True, so I am,' said the marquis, letting his arms fall by his side.

'Well, then, let us rest here, sup here, if we can, and we will start quite fit in the cool of the morning.'

'Agreed,' replied the marquis; 'but then let us pass the time in a becoming manner. I have two pistoles left, let them be given to these good fellows to drink. It is only fair that I should treat them, seeing that I am the cause of giving them so much trouble.'

He threw two pieces of money on the table of the soldiers, who cried in chorus, 'Long live M. the marquis!' The provost rose, went to post sentinels, and then repaired to the kitchen, where he ordered the best supper that could be got. The men pulled out dice and began to drink and play. The marquis hummed an air in the middle of the room, twirled his moustache, turning on his heel and looking cautiously around; then he gently drew a purse from his trousers pocket, and as the daughter of the house was coming and going, he threw his arms round her neck as if to kiss her, and whispered, slipping ten Louis into her hand—

'The key of the front door in my room, and a quart of liquor to the sentinels, and you save my life.'

The girl went backwards nearly to the door, and returning with an expressive look, made an affirmative sign with her hand. The provost returned, and two hours later supper was served. He ate and drank like a man more at home at table than in the saddle. The marquis plied him with bumpers, and sleepiness, added to the fumes of a very heady wine, caused him to repeat over and over again—

'Confound it all, marquis, I can't believe you are such a blackguard as they say you are; you seem to me a jolly good sort.'

The marquis thought he was ready to fall under the table, and was beginning to open negotiations with the daughter of the house, when, to his great disappointment, bedtime having come, the provoking provost called his sergeant, gave him instructions in an undertone, and announced that he should have the honour of conducting M. the marquis to bed, and that he should not go to bed himself before performing this duty. In fact, he posted three of his men, with torches, escorted the prisoner to his room, and left him with many profound bows.

The marquis threw himself on his bed without pulling off his boots, listening to a clock which struck nine. He heard the men come and go in the stables and in the yard.

An hour later, everybody being tired, all was perfectly still. The prisoner then rose softly, and felt about on tiptoe on the chimneypiece, on the furniture, and even in his clothes, for the key which he hoped to find. He could not find it. He could not be mistaken, nevertheless, in the tender interest of the young girl, and he could not believe that she was deceiving him. The marquis's room had a window which opened upon the street, and a door which gave access to a shabby gallery which did duty for a balcony, whence a staircase ascended to the principal rooms of the house. This gallery hung over the courtyard, being as high above it as the window was from the street. The marquis had only to jump over one side or the other: he hesitated for some time, and just as he was deciding to leap into the street, at the risk of breaking his neck, two taps were struck on the door. He jumped for joy, saying to himself as he opened, 'I am saved!' A kind of shadow glided into the room; the young girl trembled from head to foot, and could not say a word. The marquis reassured her with all sorts of caresses.

'Ah, sir,' said she, 'I am dead if we are surprised.'

'Yes,' said the marquis, 'but your fortune is made if you get me out of here.'

'God is my witness that I would with all my soul, but I have such a bad piece of news—'

She stopped, suffocated with varying emotions. The poor girl had come barefooted, for fear of making a noise, and appeared to be shivering.

'What is the matter?' impatiently asked the marquis.

'Before going to bed,' she continued, 'M. the provost has required from my father all the keys of the house, and has made him take a great oath that there are no more. My father has given him all: besides, there is a sentinel at every door; but they are very tired; I have heard them muttering and grumbling, and I have given them more wine than you told me.'

'They will sleep,' said the marquis, nowise discouraged, 'and they have already shown great respect to my rank in not nailing me up in this room.'

'There is a small kitchen garden,' continued the girl, 'on the side of the fields, fenced in only by a loose hurdle, but—'

'Where is my horse?'

'No doubt in the shed with the rest.'

'I will jump into the yard.'

'You will be killed.'

'So much the better!'

'Ah monsieur marquis, what have you done?' said the young girl with grief.

'Some foolish things! nothing worth mentioning; but my head and my honour are at stake. Let us lose no time; I have made up my mind.'

'Stay,' replied the girl, grasping his arm; 'at the left-hand corner of the yard there is a large heap of straw, the gallery hangs just over it—'

'Bravo! I shall make less noise, and do myself less mischief.' He made a step towards the door; the girl, hardly knowing what she was doing, tried to detain him; but he got loose from her and opened it. The moon was shining brightly into the yard; he heard no sound. He proceeded to the end of the wooden rail, and perceived the dungheap, which rose to a good height: the girl made the sign of the cross. The marquis listened once again, heard nothing, and mounted the rail. He was about to jump down, when by wonderful luck he heard murmurings from a deep voice. This proceeded from one of two horsemen, who were recommencing their conversation and passing between them a pint of wine. The marquis crept back to his door, holding his breath: the girl was awaiting him on the threshold.

'I told you it was not yet time,' said she.

'Have you never a knife,' said the marquis, 'to cut those rascals' throats with?'

'Wait, I entreat you, one hour, one hour only,' murmured the young girl; 'in an hour they will all be asleep.'

The girl's voice was so sweet, the arms which she stretched towards him were full of such gentle entreaty, that the marquis waited, and at the end of an hour it was the young girl's turn to tell him to start.

The marquis for the last time pressed with his mouth those lips but lately so innocent, then he half opened the door, and heard nothing this time but dogs barking far away in an otherwise silent country. He leaned over the balustrade, and saw very plainly a soldier lying prone on the straw.

'If they were to awake?' murmured the young girl in accents of anguish.

'They will not take me alive, be assured,' said the marquis.

'Adieu, then,' replied she, sobbing; 'may Heaven preserve you!'

He bestrode the balustrade, spread himself out upon it, and fell heavily on the dungheap. The young girl saw him run to the shed, hastily detach a horse, pass behind the stable wall, spur his horse in both flanks, tear across the kitchen garden, drive his horse against the hurdle, knock it down, clear it, and reach the highroad across the fields.

The poor girl remained at the end of the gallery, fixing her eyes on the sleeping sentry, and ready to disappear at the slightest movement. The noise made by spurs on the pavement and by the horse at the end of the courtyard had half awakened him. He rose, and suspecting some surprise, ran to the shed.

His horse was no longer there; the marquis, in his haste to escape, had taken the first which came to hand, and this was the soldier's. Then the soldier gave the alarm; his comrades woke up. They ran to the prisoner's room, and found it empty. The provost came from his bed in a dazed condition. The prisoner had escaped.

Then the young girl, pretending to have been roused by the noise, hindered the preparations by mislaying the saddlery, impeding the horsemen instead of helping them; nevertheless, after a quarter of an hour, all the party were galloping along the road. The provost swore like a pagan. The best horses led the way, and the sentinel, who rode the marquis's, and who had a greater interest in catching the prisoner, far outstripped his companions; he was followed by the sergeant, equally well mounted, and as the broken fence showed the line he had taken, after some minutes they were in view of him, but at a great distance. However, the marquis was losing ground; the horse he had taken was the worst in the troop, and he had pressed it as hard as it could go. Turning in the saddle, he saw the soldiers half a musket-shot off; he urged his horse more and more, tearing its sides with his spurs; but shortly the beast, completely winded, foundered; the marquis rolled with it in the dust, but when rolling over he caught hold of the holsters, which he found to contain pistols; he lay flat by the side of the horse, as if he had fainted, with a pistol at full cock in his hand. The sentinel, mounted on a valuable horse, and more than two hundred yards ahead of his serafile, came up to him. In a moment the marquis, jumping up before he had time to resist him, shot him through the head; the horseman fell, the marquis jumped up in his place without even setting foot in the stirrup, started off at a gallop, and went away like the wind, leaving fifty yards behind him the non-commissioned officer, dumbfounded with what had just passed before his eyes.

The main body of the escort galloped up, thinking that he was taken; and the provost shouted till he was hoarse, 'Do not kill him!' But they found only the sergeant, trying to restore life to his man, whose skull was shattered, and who lay dead on the spot.

As for the marquis, he was out of sight; for, fearing a fresh pursuit, he had plunged into the cross roads, along which he rode a good hour longer at full gallop. When he felt pretty sure of having shaken the police off his track, and that their bad horses could not overtake him, he determined to slacken to recruit his horse; he was walking him along a hollow lane, when he saw a peasant approaching; he asked him the road to the Bourbonnais, and flung him a crown. The man took the crown and pointed out the road, but he seemed hardly to know what he was saying, and stared at the marquis in a strange manner. The marquis shouted to him to get out of the way; but the peasant remained planted on the roadside without stirring an inch. The marquis advanced with threatening looks, and asked how he dared to stare at him like that.

'The reason is,' said the peasant, 'that you have—', and he pointed to his shoulder and his ruff.

The marquis glanced at his dress, and saw that his coat was dabbled in blood, which, added to the disorder of his clothes and the dust with which he was covered, gave him a most suspicious aspect.

'I know,' said he. 'I and my servant have been separated in a scuffle with some drunken Germans; it's only a tipsy spree, and whether I have got scratched, or whether in collaring one of these fellows I have drawn some of his blood, it all arises from the row. I don't think I am hurt a bit.' So saying, he pretended to feel all over his body.

'All the same,' he continued, 'I should not be sorry to have a wash; besides, I am dying with thirst and heat, and my horse is in no better case. Do you know where I can rest and refresh myself?'

The peasant offered to guide him to his own house, only a few yards off. His wife and children, who were working, respectfully stood aside, and went to collect what was wanted—wine, water, fruit, and a large piece of black bread. The marquis sponged his coat, drank a glass of wine, and called the people of the house, whom he questioned in an indifferent manner. He once more informed himself of the different roads leading into the Bourbonnais province, where he was going to visit a relative; of the villages, cross roads, distances; and finally he spoke of the country, the harvest, and asked what news there was.

The peasant replied, with regard to this, that it was surprising to hear of disturbances on the highway at this moment, when it was patrolled by detachments of mounted police, who had just made an important capture.

'Who is that?—' asked the marquis.

'Oh,' said the peasant, 'a nobleman who has done a lot of mischief in the country.'

'What! a nobleman in the hands of justice?'

'Just so; and he stands a good chance of losing his head.'

'Do they say what he has done?'

'Shocking things; horrid things; everything he shouldn't do. All the province is exasperated with him.'

'Do you know him?'

'No, but we all have his description.'

As this news was not encouraging, the marquis, after a few more questions, saw to his horse, patted him, threw some more money to the peasant, and disappeared in the direction pointed out.

The provost proceeded half a league farther along the road; but coming to the conclusion that pursuit was useless, he sent one of his men to headquarters, to warn all the points of exit from the province, and himself returned with his troop to the place whence he had started in the morning. The marquis had relatives in the neighbourhood, and it was quite possible that he might seek shelter with some of them. All the village ran to meet the horsemen, who were obliged to confess that they had been duped by the handsome prisoner. Different views were expressed on the event, which gave rise to much talking. The provost entered the inn, banging his fist on the furniture, and blaming everybody for the misfortune which had happened to him. The daughter of the house, at first a prey to the most grievous anxiety, had great difficulty in concealing her joy.

The provost spread his papers over the table, as if to nurse his ill-temper.

'The biggest rascal in the world!' he cried; 'I ought to have suspected him.'

'What a handsome man he was!' said the hostess.

'A consummate rascal! Do you know who he is? He is the Marquis de Saint-Maixent!'

'The Marquis de Saint-Maixent!' all cried with horror.

'Yes, the very man,' replied the provost; 'the Marquis de Saint-Maixent, accused, and indeed convicted, of coining and magic.'

'Ah!'

'Convicted of incest.'

'O my God!'

'Convicted of having strangled his wife to marry another, whose husband he had first stabbed.'

'Heaven help us!' All crossed themselves.

'Yes, good people,' continued the furious provost, 'this is the nice boy who has just escaped the king's justice!'

The host's daughter left the room, for she felt she was going to faint.

'But,' said the host, 'is there no hope of catching him again?'

'Not the slightest, if he has taken the road to the Bourbonnais; for I believe there are in that province noblemen belonging to his family who will not allow him to be rearrested.'

The fugitive was, indeed, no other than the Marquis de Saint-Maixent, accused of all the enormous crimes detailed by the provost, who by his audacious flight opened for himself an active part in the strange story which it remains to relate.

It came to pass, a fortnight after these events, that a mounted gentleman rang at the wicket gate of the chateau de Saint-Geran, at the gates of Moulins. It was late, and the servants were in no hurry to open. The stranger again pulled the bell in a masterful manner, and at length perceived a man running from the bottom of the avenue. The servant peered through the wicket, and making out in the twilight a very ill-appointed traveller, with a crushed hat, dusty clothes, and no sword, asked him what he wanted, receiving a blunt reply that the stranger wished to see the Count de Saint-Geran without any further loss of time. The servant replied that this was impossible; the other got into a passion.

'Who are you?' asked the man in livery.

'You are a very ceremonious fellow!' cried the horseman. 'Go and tell M. de Saint-Geran that his relative, the Marquis de Saint-Maixent, wishes to see him at once.'

The servant made humble apologies, and opened the wicket gate. He then walked before the marquis, called other servants, who came to help him to dismount, and ran to give his name in the count's apartments. The latter was about to sit down to supper when his relative was announced; he immediately went to receive the marquis, embraced him again and again, and gave him the most friendly and gracious reception possible. He wished then to take him into the dining-room to present him to all the family; but the marquis called his attention to the disorder of his dress, and begged for a few minutes' conversation. The count took him into his dressing-room, and had him dressed from head to foot in his own clothes, whilst they talked. The marquis then narrated a made-up story to M. de Saint-Geran relative to the accusation brought against him. This greatly impressed his relative, and gave him a secure footing in the chateau. When he had finished dressing, he followed the count, who presented him to the countess and the rest of the family.

It will now be in place to state who the inmates of the chateau were, and to relate some previous occurrences to explain subsequent ones.

The Marshal de Saint-Geran, of the illustrious house of Guiche, and governor of the Bourbonnais, had married, for his first wife, Anne de Tournon, by whom he had one son, Claude de la Guiche, and one daughter, who married the Marquis de Bouille. His wife dying, he married again with Suzanne des Epauies, who had also been previously married, being the widow of the Count de Longaunay, by whom she had Suzanne de Longaunay.

The marshal and his wife, Suzanne des Epauies, for the mutual benefit of their children by first nuptials, determined to marry them, thus sealing their own union with a double tie. Claude de Guiche, the marshal's son, married Suzanne de Longaunay.

This alliance was much to the distaste of the Marchioness de Bouille, the marshal's daughter, who found herself separated from her stepmother, and married to a man who, it was said, gave her great cause for complaint, the greatest being his threescore years and ten.

The contract of marriage between Claude de la Guiche and Suzanne de Longaunay was executed at Rouen on the 17th of February 1619; but the tender age of the bridegroom, who was then but eighteen, was the cause of his taking a tour in Italy, whence he returned after two years. The marriage was a very happy one but for one circumstance—it produced no issue. The countess could not endure a barrenness which threatened the end of a great name, the extinction of a noble race. She made vows, pilgrimages; she consulted doctors and quacks; but to no purpose.

The Marshal de Saint-Geran died on the 10th of December 1632, having the mortification of having seen no descending issue from the marriage of his son. The latter, now Count de Saint-Geran, succeeded his father in the government of the Bourbonnais, and was named Chevalier of the King's Orders.

Meanwhile the Marchioness de Bouille quarrelled with her old husband the marquis, separated from him after a scandalous divorce, and came to live at the chateau of Saint-Geran, quite at ease as to her brother's marriage, seeing that in default of heirs all his property would revert to her.

Such was the state of affairs when the Marquis de Saint-Maixent arrived at the chateau. He was young, handsome, very cunning, and very successful with women; he even made a conquest of the dowager Countess de Saint-Geran, who lived there with her children. He soon plainly saw that he might easily enter into the most intimate relations with the Marchioness de Bouille.

The Marquis de Saint-Maixent's own fortune was much impaired by his extravagance and by the exactions of the law, or rather, in plain words, he had lost it all. The marchioness was heiress presumptive to the count: he calculated that she would soon lose her own husband; in any case, the life of a septuagenarian did not much trouble a man like the marquis; he could then prevail upon the marchioness to marry him, thus giving him the command of the finest fortune in the province.

He set to work to pay his court to her, especially avoiding anything that could excite the slightest suspicion. It was, however, difficult to get on good terms with the marchioness without showing outsiders what was going on. But the marchioness, already prepossessed by the agreeable exterior of M. de Saint-Maixent, soon fell into his toils, and the unhappiness of her marriage, with the annoyances incidental to a scandalous case in the courts, left her powerless to resist his schemes. Nevertheless, they had but few opportunities of seeing one another alone: the countess innocently took a part in all their conversations; the count often came to take the marquis out hunting; the days passed in family pursuits. M. de Saint-Maixent had not so far had an opportunity of saying what a discreet woman ought to pretend not to hear; this intrigue, notwithstanding the marquis's impatience, dragged terribly.

The countess, as has been stated, had for twenty years never ceased to hope that her prayers would procure for her the grace of bearing a son to her husband. Out of sheer weariness she had given herself up to all kinds of charlatans, who at that period were well received by people of rank. On one occasion she brought from Italy a sort of astrologer, who as nearly as possible poisoned her with a horrible nostrum, and was sent back to his own country in a hurry, thanking his stars for having escaped so cheaply. This procured Madame de Saint-Geran a severe reprimand from her confessor; and, as time went on, she gradually accustomed herself to the painful conclusion that she would die childless, and cast herself into the arms of religion. The count, whose tenderness for her never failed, yet clung to the hope of an heir, and made his Will with this in view. The marchioness's hopes had become certainties, and M. de Saint-Maixent, perfectly tranquil on this head, thought only of forwarding his suit with Madame de Bouille, when, at the end of the month of November 1640, the Count de Saint-Geran was obliged to repair to Paris in great haste on pressing duty.

The countess, who could not bear to be separated from

her husband, took the family advice as to accompanying him. The marquis, delighted at an opportunity which left him almost alone in the chateau with Madame de Bouille, painted the journey to Paris in the most attractive colours, and said all he could to decide her to go. The marchioness, for her part, worked very quietly to the same end; it was more than was needed. It was settled that the countess should go with M. de Saint-Geran. She soon made her preparations, and a few days later they set off on the journey together.

The marquis had no fears about declaring his passion; the conquest of Madame de Bouille gave him no trouble; he affected the most violent love, and she responded in the same terms. All their time was spent in excursions and walks from which the servants were excluded; the lovers, always together, passed whole days in some retired part of the park, or shut up in their apartments. It was impossible for these circumstances not to cause gossip among an army of servants, against whom they had to keep incessantly on their guard; and this naturally happened.

The marchioness soon found herself obliged to make confidantes of the sisters Quinet, her maids; she had no difficulty in gaining their support, for the girls were greatly attached to her. This was the first step of shame for Madame de Bouille, and the first step of corruption for herself and her paramour, who soon found themselves entangled in the blackest of plots. Moreover, there was at the chateau de Saint-Geran a tall, spare, yellow, stupid man, just intelligent enough to perform, if not to conceive, a bad action, who was placed in authority over the domestics; he was a common peasant whom the old marshal had deigned to notice, and whom the count had by degrees promoted to the service of major-domo on account of his long service in the house, and because he had seen him there since he himself was a child; he would not take him away as body servant, fearing that his notions of service would not do for Paris, and left him to the superintendence of the household. The marquis had a quiet talk with this man, took his measure, warped his mind as he wished, gave him some money, and acquired him body and soul. These different agents undertook to stop the chatter of the servants' hall, and thenceforward the lovers could enjoy free intercourse.

One evening, as the Marquis de Saint-Maixent was at supper in company with the marchioness, a loud knocking was heard at the gate of the chateau, to which they paid no great attention. This was followed by the appearance of a courier who had come post haste from Paris; he entered the courtyard with a letter from the Count de Saint-Geran for M. the marquis; he was announced and introduced, followed by nearly all the household. The marquis asked the meaning of all this, and dismissed all the following with a wave of the hand; but the courier explained that M. the count desired that the letter in his hands should be read before everyone. The marquis opened it without replying, glanced over it, and read it out loud without the slightest alteration: the count announced to his good relations and to all his household that the countess had indicated positive symptoms of pregnancy; that hardly had she arrived in Paris when she suffered from fainting fits, nausea, retching, that she bore with joy these premonitory indications, which were no longer a matter of doubt to the physicians, nor to anyone; that for his part he was overwhelmed with joy at this event, which was the crowning stroke to all his wishes; that he desired the chateau to share his satisfaction by indulging in all kinds of gaieties; and that so far as other matters were concerned they could remain as they were till the return of himself and the countess, which the letter would precede only a few days, as he was going to transport her in a litter for greater safety. Then followed the specification of certain sums of money to be distributed among the servants.

The servants uttered cries of joy; the marquis and marchioness exchanged a look, but a very troublous one; they, however, restrained themselves so far as to simulate a great satisfaction, and the marquis brought himself to congratulate the servants on their attachment to their master and mistress. After this they were left alone, looking very serious, while crackers exploded and violins resounded under the windows. For some time they preserved silence, the first thought which occurred to both being that the count and countess had allowed themselves to be deceived by trifling symptoms, that people had wished to flatter their hopes, that it was impossible for a constitution to change so suddenly after twenty years, and that it was a case of simulative pregnancy. This opinion gaining strength in their minds made them somewhat calmer.

The next day they took a walk side by side in a solitary path in the park and discussed the chances of their situation. M. de Saint-Maixent brought before the marchioness the enormous injury which this event would bring them. He then said that even supposing the news to be true, there were many rocks ahead to be weathered before the succession could be pronounced secure.

'The child may die,' he said at last.

And he uttered some sinister expressions on the slight damage caused by the loss of a puny creature without mind, interest, or consequence; nothing, he said, but a bit of ill-organised matter, which only came into the world to ruin so considerable a person as the marchioness.

'But what is the use of tormenting ourselves?' he went on impatiently; 'the countess is not pregnant, nor can she be.'

A gardener working near them overheard this part of the conversation, but as they walked away from him he could not hear any more.

who went beside themselves with joy not one remarked the disappointment which overspread her soul. Every day she saw the marquis, who did all he could to increase her regret, and incessantly stirred up her ill-humour by repeating that the count and countess were triumphing over her misfortune, and insinuating that they were importing a supposititious child to disinherit her. As usual both in private and political affairs, he began by corrupting the marchioness's religious views, to pervert her into crime. The marquis was one of those libertines so rare at that time, a period less unhappy than is generally believed, who made science dependent upon atheism. It is remarkable that great criminals of this epoch, Sainte-Croix for instance, and Exili, the gloomy poisoner, were the first unbelievers, and that they preceded the learned of the following age both in philosophy and in the exclusive study of physical science, in which they included that of poisons. Passion, interest, hatred fought the marquis's battles in the heart of Madame de Bouille; she readily lent herself to everything that M. de Saint-Maixent wished.

The Marquis de Saint-Maixent had a confidential servant, cunning, insolent, resourceful, whom he had brought from his estates, a servant well suited to such a master, whom he sent on errands frequently into the neighbourhood of Saint-Geran.

One evening, as the marquis was about to go to bed, this man, returning from one of his expeditions, entered his room, where he remained for a long time, telling him that he had at length found what he wanted, and giving him a small piece of paper which contained several names of places and persons.

Next morning, at daybreak, the marquis caused two of his horses to be saddled, pretended that he was summoned home on pressing business, foresaw that he should be absent for three or four days, made his excuses to the count, and set off at full gallop, followed by his servant.

A few days later, some outriders, sent before him by the count, entered the chateau, saying that their master and mistress were close at hand. In fact, they were promptly followed by brakes and travelling-carriages, and at length the countess's litter was descried, which M. de Saint-Geran, on horse back, had never lost sight of during the journey. It was a triumphal reception: all the peasants had left their work, and filled the air with shouts of welcome; the servants ran to meet their mistress; the ancient retainers wept for joy at seeing the count so happy and in the hope that his noble qualities might be perpetuated in his heir. The marquis and Madame de Bouille did their best to tune up to the pitch of this hilarity.

The dowager countess, who had arrived at the chateau the same day, unable to convince herself as to this news, had the pleasure of satisfying herself respecting it. The count and countess were much beloved in the Bourbonnais province; this event caused therein a general satisfaction, particularly in the numerous houses attached to them by consanguinity. Within a few days of their return, more than twenty ladies of quality flocked to visit them in great haste, to show the great interest they took in this pregnancy. All these ladies, on one occasion or another, convinced themselves as to its genuineness, and many of them, carrying the subject still further, in a joking manner which pleased the countess, dubbed themselves prophetesses, and predicted the birth of a boy. The usual symptoms incidental to the situation left no room for doubt: the country physicians were all agreed. The count kept one of these physicians in the chateau for two months, and spoke to the Marquis of Saint-Maixent of his intention of procuring a good midwife, on the same terms. Finally, the dowager countess, who was to be sponsor, ordered at a great expense a magnificent store of baby linen, which she desired to present at the birth.

The marchioness devoured her rage, and among the persons

They slept that night at an inn on the road to Auvergne, to put off the scent any persons who might recognise them; then, following cross-country roads, they arrived after two days at a large hamlet, which they had seemed to have passed far to their left.

In this hamlet was a woman who practised the avocation of midwife, and was known as such in the neighbourhood, but who had, it was said, mysterious and infamous secrets for those who paid her well. Further, she drew a good income from the influence which her art gave her over credulous people. It was all in her line to cure the king's evil, compound philtres and love potions; she was useful in a variety of ways to girls who could afford to pay her; she was a lovers' go-between, and even practised sorcery for country folk. She played her cards so well, that the only persons privy to her misdeeds were unfortunate creatures who had as strong an interest as herself in keeping them profoundly secret; and as her terms were very high, she lived comfortably enough in a house her own property, and entirely alone, for greater security. In a general way, she was considered skilful in her ostensible profession, and was held in estimation by many persons of rank. This woman's name was Louise Goillard.

Alone one evening after curfew, she heard a loud knocking at the door of her house. Accustomed to receive visits at all hours, she took her lamp without hesitation, and opened the door. An armed man, apparently much agitated, entered the room. Louise Goillard, in a great fright, fell into a chair; this man was the Marquis de Saint-Maixent.

'Calm yourself, good woman,' said the stranger, panting and stammering; 'be calm, I beg; for it is I, not you, who have any cause for emotion. I am not a brigand, and far from your having anything to fear, it is I, on the contrary, who am come to beg for your assistance.'

He threw his cloak into a corner, unbuckled his waistbelt, and laid aside his sword. Then falling into a chair, he said—

'First of all, let me rest a little.'

The marquis wore a travelling-dress; but although he had not stated his name, Louise Goillard saw at a glance that he was a very different person from what she had thought, and that, on the contrary, he was some fine gentleman who had come on his love affairs.

'I beg you to excuse,' said she, 'a fear which is insulting to you. You came in so hurriedly that I had not time to see whom I was talking to. My house is rather lonely; I am alone; ill-disposed people might easily take advantage of these circumstances to plunder a poor woman who has little enough to lose. The times are so bad! You seem tired. Will you inhale some essence?'

'Give me only a glass of water.'

Louise Goillard went into the adjoining room, and returned with an ewer. The marquis affected to rinse his lips, and said—

'I come from a great distance on a most important matter. Be assured that I shall be properly grateful for your services.'

He felt in his pocket, and pulled out a purse, which he rolled between his fingers.

'In the first place; you must swear to the greatest secrecy.'

'There is no need of that with us,' said Louise Goillard; 'that is the first condition of our craft.'

'I must have more express guarantees, and your oath that you will reveal to no one in the world what I am going to confide to you.'

'I give you my word, then, since you demand it; but I repeat that this is superfluous; you do not know me.'

'Consider that this is a most serious matter, that I am as it were placing my head in your hands, and that I would lose my life a thousand times rather than see this mystery unravelled.'

'Consider also,' bluntly replied the midwife, 'that we

ourselves are primarily interested in all the secrets entrusted to us; that an indiscretion would destroy all confidence in us, and that there are even cases—You may speak.'

When the marquis had reassured her as to himself by this preface, he continued: 'I know that you are a very able woman.'

'I could indeed wish to be one, to serve you.'

'That you have pushed the study of your art to its utmost limits.'

'I fear they have been flattering your humble servant.'

'And that your studies have enabled you to predict the future.'

'That is all nonsense.'

'It is true; I have been told so.'

'You have been imposed upon.'

'What is the use of denying it and refusing to do me a service?'

Louise Goillard defended herself long: she could not understand a man of this quality believing in fortune-telling, which she practised only with low-class people and rich farmers; but the marquis appeared so earnest that she knew not what to think.

'Listen,' said he, 'it is no use dissembling with me, I know all. Be easy; we are playing a game in which you are laying one against a thousand; moreover, here is something on account to compensate you for the trouble I am giving.'

He laid a pile of gold on the table. The matron weakly owned that she had sometimes attempted astrological combinations which were not always fortunate, and that she had been only induced to do so by the fascination of the phenomena of science. The secret of her guilty practices was drawn from her at the very outset of her defence.

'That being so,' replied the marquis, 'you must be already aware of the situation in which I find myself; you must know that, hurried away by a blind and ardent passion, I have betrayed the confidence of an old lady and violated the laws of hospitality by seducing her daughter in her own house; that matters have come to a crisis, and that this noble damsel, whom I love to distraction, being pregnant, is on the point of losing her life and honour by the discovery of her fault, which is mine.'

The matron replied that nothing could be ascertained about a person except from private questions; and to further impose upon the marquis, she fetched a kind of box marked with figures and strange emblems. Opening this, and putting together certain figures which it contained, she declared that what the marquis had told her was true, and that his situation was a most melancholy one. She added, in order to frighten him, that he was threatened by still more serious misfortunes than those which had already overtaken him, but that it was easy to anticipate and obviate these mischances by new consultations.

'Madame,' replied the marquis, 'I fear only one thing in the world, the dishonour of the woman I love. Is there no method of remedying the usual embarrassment of a birth?'

'I know of none,' said the matron.

'The young lady has succeeded in concealing her condition; it would be easy for her confinement to take place privately.'

'She has already risked her life; and I cannot consent to be mixed up in this affair, for fear of the consequences.'

'Could not, for instance,' said the marquis, 'a confinement be effected without pain?'

'I don't know about that, but this I do know, that I shall take very good care not to practise any method contrary to the laws of nature.'

'You are deceiving me: you are acquainted with this method, you have already practised it upon a certain person whom I could name to you.'

'Who has dared to calumniate me thus? I operate only after

the decision of the Faculty. God forbid that I should be stoned by all the physicians, and perhaps expelled from France!'

'Will you then let me die of despair? If I were capable of making a bad use of your secrets, I could have done so long ago, for I know them. In Heaven's name, do not dissimulate any longer, and tell me how it is possible to stifle the pangs of labour. Do you want more gold? Here it is.' And he threw more Louis on the table.

'Stay,' said the matron: 'there is perhaps a method which I think I have discovered, and which I have never employed, but I believe it efficacious.'

'But if you have never employed it, it may be dangerous, and risk the life of the lady whom I love.'

'When I say never, I mean that I have tried it once, and most successfully. Be at your ease.'

'Ah!' cried the marquis, 'you have earned my everlasting gratitude! But,' continued he, 'if we could anticipate the confinement itself, and remove from henceforth the symptoms of pregnancy?'

'Oh, sir, that is a great crime you speak of!'

'Alas!' continued the marquis, as if speaking to himself in a fit of intense grief; 'I had rather lose a dear child, the pledge of our love, than bring into the world an unhappy creature which might possibly cause its mother's death.'

'I pray you, sir, let no more be said on the subject; it is a horrible crime even to think of such a thing.'

'But what is to be done? Is it better to destroy two persons and perhaps kill a whole family with despair? Oh, madame, I entreat you, extricate us from this extremity!'

The marquis buried his face in his hands, and sobbed as though he were weeping copiously.

'Your despair grievously affects me,' said the matron; 'but consider that for a woman of my calling it is a capital offence.'

'What are you talking about? Do not our mystery, our safety, and our credit come in first?'

'They can never get at you till after the death and dishonour of all that is dear to me in the world.'

'I might then, perhaps. But in this case you must insure me against legal complications, fines, and procure me a safe exit from the kingdom.'

'Ah! that is my affair. Take my whole fortune! Take my life!'

And he threw the whole purse on the table.

'In this case, and solely to extricate you from the extreme danger in which I see you placed, I consent to give you a decoction, and certain instructions, which will instantly relieve the lady from her burden. She must use the greatest precaution, and study to carry out exactly what I am about to tell you. My God! only such desperate occasions as this one could induce me to—Here—'

She took a flask from the bottom of a cupboard, and continued—

'Here is a liquor which never fails.'

'Oh, madame, you save my honour, which is dearer to me than life! But this is not enough: tell me what use I am to make of this liquor, and in what doses I am to administer it.'

'The patient,' replied the midwife, 'must take one spoonful the first day; the second day two; the third—'

'You will obey me to the minutest particular?'

'I swear it.'

'Let us start, then.'

She asked but for time to pack a little linen, put things in order, then fastened her doors, and left the house with the marquis. A quarter of an hour later they were galloping through the night, without her knowing where the marquis was taking her.

The marquis reappeared three days later at the chateau,

finding the count's family as he had left them—that is to say, intoxicated with hope, and counting the weeks, days, and hours before the accouchement of the countess. He excused his hurried departure on the ground of the importance of the business which had summoned him away; and speaking of his journey at table, he related a story current in the country whence he came, of a surprising event which he had all but witnessed. It was the case of a lady of quality who suddenly found herself in the most dangerous pangs of labour. All the skill of the physicians who had been summoned proved futile; the lady was at the point of death; at last, in sheer despair, they summoned a midwife of great repute among the peasantry, but whose practice did not include the gentry. From the first treatment of this woman, who appeared modest and diffident to a degree, the pains ceased as if by enchantment; the patient fell into an indefinable calm languor, and after some hours was delivered of a beautiful infant; but after this was attacked by a violent fever which brought her to death's door. They then again had recourse to the doctors, notwithstanding the opposition of the master of the house, who had confidence in the matron. The doctors' treatment only made matters worse. In this extremity they again called in the midwife, and at the end of three weeks the lady was miraculously restored to life, thus, added the marquis, establishing the reputation of the matron, who had sprung into such vogue in the town where she lived and the neighbouring country that nothing else was talked about.

This story made a great impression on the company, on account of the condition of the countess; the dowager added that it was very wrong to ridicule these humble country experts, who often through observation and experience discovered secrets which proud doctors were unable to unravel with all their studies. Hereupon the count cried out that this midwife must be sent for, as she was just the kind of woman they wanted. After this other matters were talked about, the marquis changing the conversation; he had gained his point in quietly introducing the thin end of the wedge of his design.

After dinner, the company walked on the terrace. The countess dowager not being able to walk much on account of her advanced age, the countess and Madame de Bouille took chairs beside her. The count walked up and down with M. de Saint-Maixent. The marquis naturally asked how things had been going on during his absence, and if Madame de Saint-Geran had suffered any inconvenience, for her pregnancy had become the most important affair in the household, and hardly anything else was talked about.

'By the way,' said the count, 'you were speaking just now of a very skilful midwife; would it not be a good step to summon her?'

'I think,' replied the marquis, 'that it would be an excellent selection, for I do not suppose there is one in this neighbourhood to compare to her.'

'I have a great mind to send for her at once, and to keep her about the countess, whose constitution she will be all the better acquainted with if she studies it beforehand. Do you know where I can send for her?'

'Faith,' said the marquis, 'she lives in a village, but I don't know which.'

'But at least you know her name?'

'I can hardly remember it. Louise Boyard, I think, or Polliard, one or the other.'

'How! have you not even retained the name?'

'I heard the story, that's all. Who the deuce can keep a name in his head which he hears in such a chance fashion?'

'But did the condition of the countess never occur to you?'

'It was so far away that I did not suppose you would send

such a distance. I thought you were already provided.'

'How can we set about to find her?'

'If that is all, I have a servant who knows people in that part of the country, and who knows how to go about things: if you like, he shall go in quest of her.'

'If I like? This very moment.'

The same evening the servant started on his errand with the count's instructions, not forgetting those of his master. He went at full speed. It may readily be supposed that he had not far to seek the woman he was to bring back with him; but he purposely kept away for three days, and at the end of this time Louise Goillard was installed in the chateau.

She was a woman of plain and severe exterior, who at once inspired confidence in everyone. The plots of the marquis and Madame de Bouille thus throve with most baneful success; but an accident happened which threatened to nullify them, and, by causing a great disaster, to prevent a crime.

The countess, passing into her apartments, caught her foot in a carpet, and fell heavily on the floor. At the cries of a footman all the household was astir. The countess was carried to bed; the most intense alarm prevailed; but no bad consequences followed this accident, which produced only a further succession of visits from the neighbouring gentry. This happened about the end of the seventh month.

At length the moment of accouchement came. Everything had long before been arranged for the delivery, and nothing remained to be done. The marquis had employed all this time in strengthening Madame de Bouille against her scruples. He often saw Louise Goillard in private, and gave her his instructions; but he perceived that the corruption of Baulieu, the house steward, was an essential factor. Baulieu was already half gained over by the interviews of the year preceding; a large sum of ready money and many promises did the rest. This wretch was not ashamed to join a plot against a master to whom he owed everything. The marchioness for her part, and always under the instigation of M. de Saint-Maixent, secured matters all round by bringing into the abominable plot the Quinet girls, her maids; so that there was nothing but treason and conspiracy against this worthy family among their upper servants, usually styled confidential. Thus, having prepared matters, the conspirators awaited the event.

On the 16th of August the Countess de Saint-Geran was overtaken by the pangs of labour in the chapel of the chateau, where she was hearing mass. They carried her to her room before mass was over, her women ran around her, and the countess dowager with her own hands arranged on her head a cap of the pattern worn by ladies about to be confined—a cap which is not usually removed till some time later.

The pains recurred with terrible intensity. The count wept at his wife's cries. Many persons were present. The dowager's two daughters by her second marriage, one of whom, then sixteen years of age, afterwards married the Duke de Ventadour and was a party to the lawsuit, wished to be present at this accouchement, which was to perpetuate by a new scion an illustrious race near extinction. There were also Dame Saligny, sister of the late Marshal Saint-Geran, the Marquis de Saint-Maixent, and the Marchioness de Bouille.

Everything seemed to favour the projects of these last two persons, who took an interest in the event of a very different character from that generally felt. As the pains produced no result, and the accouchement was of the most difficult nature, while the countess was near the last extremity, expresses were sent to all the neighbouring parishes to offer prayers for the mother and the child; the Holy Sacrament was elevated in the churches at Moulins.

The midwife attended to everything herself. She maintained

that the countess would be more comfortable if her slightest desires were instantly complied with. The countess herself never spoke a word, only interrupting the gloomy silence by heart-rending cries. All at once, Madame de Bouille, who affected to be bustling about, pointed out that the presence of so many persons was what hindered the countess's accouchement, and, assuming an air of authority justified by fictitious tenderness, said that everyone must retire, leaving the patient in the hands of the persons who were absolutely necessary to her, and that, to remove any possible objections, the countess dowager her mother must set the example. The opportunity was made use of to remove the count from this harrowing spectacle, and everyone followed the countess dowager. Even the countess's own maids were not allowed to remain, being sent on errands which kept them out of the way. This further reason was given, that the eldest being scarcely fifteen, they were too young to be present on such an occasion. The only persons remaining by the bedside were the Marchioness de Bouille, the midwife, and the two Quinet girls; the countess was thus in the hands of her most cruel enemies.

It was seven o'clock in the evening; the labours continued; the elder Quinet girl held the patient by the hand to soothe her. The count and the dowager sent incessantly to know the news. They were told that everything was going on well, and that shortly their wishes would be accomplished; but none of the servants were allowed to enter the room.

Three hours later, the midwife declared that the countess could not hold out any longer unless she got some rest. She made her swallow a liquor which was introduced into her mouth by spoonfuls. The countess fell into so deep a sleep that she seemed to be dead. The younger Quinet girl thought for a moment that they had killed her, and wept in a corner of the room, till Madame de Bouille reassured her.

During this frightful night a shadowy figure prowled in the corridors, silently patrolled the rooms, and came now and then to the door of the bedroom, where he conferred in a low tone with the midwife and the Marchioness de Bouille. This was the Marquis de Saint-Maixent, who gave his orders, encouraged his people, watched over every point of his plot, himself a prey to the agonies of nervousness which accompany the preparations for a great crime.

The dowager countess, owing to her great age, had been compelled to take some rest. The count sat up, worn out with fatigue, in a downstairs room hard by that in which they were compassing the ruin of all most dear to him in the world.

The countess, in her profound lethargy, gave birth, without being aware of it, to a boy, who thus fell on his entry into the world into the hands of his enemies, his mother powerless to defend him by her cries and tears. The door was half opened, and a man who was waiting outside brought in; this was the major-domo Baulieu.

The midwife, pretending to afford the first necessary cares to the child, had taken it into a corner. Baulieu watched her movements, and springing upon her, pinioned her arms. The wretched woman dug her nails into the child's head. He snatched it from her, but the poor infant for long bore the marks of her claws.

Possibly the Marchioness de Bouille could not nerve herself to the commission of so great a crime; but it seems more probable that the steward prevented the destruction of the child under the orders of M. de Saint-Maixent. The theory is that the marquis, mistrustful of the promise made him by Madame de Bouille to marry him after the death of her husband, desired to keep the child to oblige her to keep her word, under threats of getting him acknowledged, if she proved faithless to him. No other adequate reason can be conjectured to determine a man of his character to take such great care of his victim.

Baulieu swaddled the child immediately, put it in a basket, hid it under his cloak, and went with his prey to find the marquis; they conferred together for some time, after which the house steward passed by a postern gate into the moat, thence to a terrace by which he reached a bridge leading into the park. This park had twelve gates, and he had the keys of all. He mounted a blood horse which he had left waiting behind a wall, and started off at full gallop. The same day he passed through the village of Escherolles, a league distant from Saint-Geran, where he stopped at the house of a nurse, wife of a glovemaker named Claude. This peasant woman gave her breast to the child; but the steward, not daring to stay in a village so near Saint-Geran, crossed the river Allier at the port de la Chaise, and calling at the house of a man named Boucaud, the good wife suckled the child for the second time; he then continued his journey in the direction of Auvergne.

The heat was excessive, his horse was done up, the child seemed uneasy. A carrier's cart passed him going to Riom; it was owned by a certain Paul Boithion of the town of Aigueperce, a common carrier on the road. Baulieu went alongside to put the child in the cart, which he entered himself, carrying the infant on his knees. The horse followed, fastened by the bridle to the back of the cart.

In the conversation which he held with this man, Baulieu said that he should not take so much care of the child did it not belong to the most noble house in the Bourbonnais. They reached the village of Che at midday. The mistress of the house where he put up, who was nursing an infant, consented to give some of her milk to the child. The poor creature was covered with blood; she warmed some water, stripped off its swaddling linen, washed it from head to foot, and swathed it up again more neatly.

The carrier then took them to Riom. When they got there, Baulieu got rid of him by giving a false meeting-place for their departure; left in the direction of the abbey of Lavoine, and reached the village of Descoutoux, in the mountains, between Lavoine and Thiers. The Marchioness de Bouille had a chateau there where she occasionally spent some time.

The child was nursed at Descoutoux by Gabrielle Moini, who was paid a month in advance; but she only kept it a week or so, because they refused to tell her the father and mother and to refer her to a place where she might send reports of her charge. This woman having made these reasons public, no nurse could be found to take charge of the child, which was removed from the village of Descoutoux. The persons who removed it took the highroad to Burgundy, crossing a densely wooded country, and here they lost their way.

The above particulars were subsequently proved by the nurses, the carrier, and others who made legal depositions. They are stated at length here, as they proved very important in the great lawsuit. The compilers of the case, into which we search for information, have however omitted to tell us how the absence of the major-domo was accounted for at the castle; probably the far-sighted marquis had got an excuse ready.

The countess's state of drowsiness continued till daybreak. She woke bathed in blood, completely exhausted, but yet with a sensation of comfort which convinced her that she had been delivered from her burden. Her first words were about her child; she wished to see it, kiss it; she asked where it was. The midwife coolly told her, whilst the girls who were by were filled with amazement at her audacity, that she had not been confined at all. The countess maintained the contrary, and as she grew very excited, the midwife strove to calm her, assuring her that in any case her delivery could not be long protracted, and that, judging from all the indications of the night, she would give birth to a boy. This promise comforted the count and the countess dowager, but failed to satisfy the countess, who insisted that a child had been born.

The same day a scullery-maid met a woman going to the water's edge in the castle moat, with a parcel in her arms. She recognised the midwife, and asked what she was carrying and where she was going so early. The latter replied that she was very inquisitive, and that it was nothing at all; but the girl, laughingly pretending to be angry at this answer, pulled open one of the ends of the parcel before the midwife had time to stop her, and exposed to view some linen soaked in blood.

'Madame has been confined, then?' she said to the matron.

'No,' replied she briskly, 'she has not.'

The girl was unconvinced, and said, 'How do you mean that she has not, when madame the marchioness, who was there, says she has?' The matron in great confusion replied, 'She must have a very long tongue, if she said so.'

The girl's evidence was later found most important.

The countess's uneasiness made her worse the next day. She implored with sighs and tears at least to be told what had become of her child, steadily maintaining that she was not mistaken when she assured them that she had given birth to one. The midwife with great effrontery told her that the new moon was unfavourable to childbirth, and that she must wait for the wane, when it would be easier as matters were already prepared.

Invalids' fancies do not obtain much credence; still, the persistence of the countess would have convinced everyone in the long run, had not the dowager said that she remembered at the end of the ninth month of one of her own pregnancies she had all the premonitory symptoms of lying in, but they proved false, and in fact the accouchement took place three months later.

This piece of news inspired great confidence. The marquis and Madame de Bouille did all in their power to confirm it, but the countess obstinately refused to listen to it, and her passionate transports of grief gave rise to the greatest anxiety. The midwife, who knew not how to gain time, and was losing all hope in face of the countess's persistence, was almost frightened out of her wits; she entered into medical details, and finally said that some violent exercise must be taken to induce labour. The countess, still unconvinced, refused to obey this order; but the count, the dowager, and all the family entreated her so earnestly that she gave way.

They put her in a close carriage, and drove her a whole day over ploughed fields, by the roughest and hardest roads. She was so shaken that she lost the power of breathing; it required all the strength of her constitution to support this barbarous treatment in the delicate condition of a lady so recently confined. They put her to bed again after this cruel drive, and seeing that nobody took her view, she threw herself into the arms of Providence, and consoled herself by religion; the midwife administered violent remedies to deprive her of milk; she got over all these attempts to murder her, and slowly got better.

Time, which heals the deepest affliction, gradually soothed that of the countess; her grief nevertheless burst out periodically on the slightest cause; but eventually it died out, till the following events rekindled it.

There had been in Paris a fencing-master who used to boast that he had a brother in the service of a great house. This fencing-master had married a certain Marie Pigoreau, daughter of an actor. He had recently died in poor circumstances, leaving her a widow with two children. This woman Pigoreau did not enjoy the best of characters, and no one knew how she made a living, when all at once, after some short absences from home and visit from a man who came in the evening, his face muffled in his cloak, she launched out into a more expensive style of living; the neighbours saw in her house costly clothes, fine swaddling-clothes, and at last it became known that she was nursing a strange child.

About the same time it also transpired that she had a deposit of two thousand livres in the hands of a grocer in the quarter, named Raguenet; some days later, as the child's baptism had doubtless been put off for fear of betraying his origin, Pigoreau had him christened at St. Jean en Greve. She did not invite any of the neighbours to the function, and gave parents' names of her own choosing at the church. For godfather she selected the parish sexton, named Paul Marmiou, who gave the child the name of Bernard. La Pigoreau remained in a confessional during the ceremony, and gave the man ten sou. The godmother was Jeanne Chevalier, a poor woman of the parish.

The entry in the register was as follows:—

> 'On the seventh day of March one thousand six hundred and forty-two was baptized Bernard, son of...and...his godfather being Paul Marmiou, day labourer and servant of this parish, and his godmother Jeanne Chevalier, widow of Pierre Thibou.'

A few days afterwards la Pigoreau put out the child to nurse in the village of Torcy en Brie, with a woman who had been her godmother, whose husband was called Paillard. She gave out that it was a child of quality which had been entrusted to her, and that she should not hesitate, if such a thing were necessary, to save its life by the loss of one of her own children. The nurse did not keep it long, because she fell ill; la Pigoreau went to fetch the child away, lamenting this accident, and further saying that she regretted it all the more, as the nurse would have earned enough to make her comfortable for the rest of her life. She put the infant out again in the same village, with the widow of a peasant named Marc Peguin. The monthly wage was regularly paid, and the child brought up as one of rank. La Pigoreau further told the woman that it was the son of a great nobleman, and would later make the fortunes of those who served him. An elderly man, whom the people supposed to be the child's father, but who Pigoreau assured them was her brother-in-law, often came to see him.

When the child was eighteen months old, la Pigoreau took him away and weaned him. Of the two by her husband the elder was called Antoine, the second would have been called Henri if he had lived; but he was born on the 9th of August 1639, after the death of his father, who was killed in June of the same year, and died shortly after his birth. La Pigoreau thought fit to give the name and condition of this second son to the stranger, and thus bury for ever the secret of his birth. With this end in view, she left the quarter where she lived, and removed to conceal herself in another parish where she was not known. The child was brought up under the name and style of Henri, second son of la Pigoreau, till he was two and a half years of age; but at this time, whether she was not engaged to keep it any longer, or whether she had spent the two thousand livres deposited with the grocer Raguenet, and could get no more from the principals, she determined to get rid of it.

Her gossips used to tell this woman that she cared but little for her eldest son, because she was very confident of the second one making his fortune, and that if she were obliged to give up one of them, she had better keep the younger, who was a beautiful boy. To this she would reply that the matter did not depend upon her; that the boy's godfather was an uncle in good circumstances, who would not charge himself with any other child. She often mentioned this uncle, her brother-in-law, she said, who was major-domo in a great house.

One morning, the hall porter at the hotel de Saint-Geran

came to Baulieu and told him that a woman carrying a child was asking for him at the wicket gate; this Baulieu was, in fact, the brother of the fencing master, and godfather to Pigoreau's second son. It is now supposed that he was the unknown person who had placed the child of quality with her, and who used to go and see him at his nurse's. La Pigoreau gave him a long account of her situation. The major-domo took the child with some emotion, and told la Pigoreau to wait his answer a short distance off, in a place which he pointed out.

Baulieu's wife made a great outcry at the first proposal of an increase of family; but he succeeded in pacifying her by pointing out the necessities of his sister-in-law, and how easy and inexpensive it was to do this good work in such a house as the count's. He went to his master and mistress to ask permission to bring up this child in their hotel; a kind of feeling entered into the charge he was undertaking which in some measure lessened the weight on his conscience.

The count and countess at first opposed this project; telling him that having already five children he ought not to burden himself with any more, but he petitioned so earnestly that he obtained what he wanted. The countess wished to see it, and as she was about to start for Moulins she ordered it to be put in her women's coach; when it was shown her, she cried out, 'What a lovely child!' The boy was fair, with large blue eyes and very regular features. She gave him a hundred caresses, which the child returned very prettily. She at once took a great fancy to him, and said to Baulieu, 'I shall not put him in my women's coach; I shall put him in my own.'

After they arrived at the chateau of Saint-Geran, her affection for Henri, the name retained by the child, increased day by day. She often contemplated him with sadness, then embraced him with tenderness, and kept him long on her bosom. The count shared this affection for the supposed nephew of Baulieu, who was adopted, so to speak, and brought up like a child of quality.

The Marquis de Saint-Maixent and Madame de Bouille had not married, although the old Marquis de Bouille had long been dead. It appeared that they had given up this scheme. The marchioness no doubt felt scruples about it, and the marquis was deterred from marriage by his profligate habits. It is moreover supposed that other engagements and heavy bribes compensated the loss he derived from the marchioness's breach of faith.

He was a man about town at that period, and was making love to the demoiselle Jacqueline de la Garde; he had succeeded in gaining her affections, and brought matters to such a point that she no longer refused her favours except on the grounds of her pregnancy and the danger of an indiscretion. The marquis then offered to introduce to her a matron who could deliver women without the pangs of labour, and who had a very successful practice. The same Jacqueline de la Garde further gave evidence at the trial that M. de Saint-Maixent had often boasted, as of a scientific intrigue, of having spirited away the son of a governor of a province and grandson of a marshal of France; that he spoke of the Marchioness de Bouille, said that he had made her rich, and that it was to him she owed her great wealth; and further, that one day having taken her to a pretty country seat which belonged to him, she praised its beauty, saying 'c'etait un beau lieu'; he replied by a pun on a man's name, saying that he knew another Baulieu who had enabled him to make a fortune of five hundred thousand crowns. He also said to Jadelon, sieur de la Barbesange, when posting with him from Paris, that the Countess de Saint-Geran had been delivered of a son who was in his power.

The marquis had not seen Madame de Bouille for a long time; a common danger reunited them. They had both learned with terror the presence of Henri at the hotel de Saint-Geran.

They consulted about this; the marquis undertook to cut the danger short. However, he dared put in practice nothing overtly against the child, a matter still more difficult just then, inasmuch as some particulars of his discreditable adventures had leaked out, and the Saint-Geran family received him more than coldly.

Baulieu, who witnessed every day the tenderness of the count and countess for the boy Henri, had been a hundred times on the point of giving himself up and confessing everything. He was torn to pieces with remorse. Remarks escaped him which he thought he might make without ulterior consequences; seeing the lapse of time, but they were noted and commented on. Sometimes he would say that he held in his hand the life and honour of Madame the Marchioness de Bouille; sometimes that the count and countess had more reasons than they knew of for loving Henri. One day he put a case of conscience to a confessor, thus: 'Whether a man who had been concerned in the abduction of a child could not satisfy his conscience by restoring him to his father and mother without telling them who he was?' What answer the confessor made is not known, but apparently it was not what the major-domo wanted. He replied to a magistrate of Moulins, who congratulated him on having a nephew whom his masters overburdened with kind treatment, that they ought to love him, since he was nearly related to them.

These remarks were noticed by others than those principally concerned. One day a wine merchant came to propose to Baulieu the purchase of a pipe of Spanish wine, of which he gave him a sample bottle; in the evening he was taken violently ill. They carried him to bed, where he writhed, uttering horrible cries. One sole thought possessed him when his sufferings left him a lucid interval, and in his agony he repeated over and over again that he wished to implore pardon from the count and countess for a great injury which he had done them. The people round about him told him that was a trifle, and that he ought not to let it embitter his last moments, but he begged so piteously that he got them to promise that they should be sent for.

The count thought it was some trifling irregularity, some misappropriation in the house accounts; and fearing to hasten the death of the sufferer by the shame of the confession of a fault, he sent word that he heartily forgave him, that he might die tranquil, and refused to see him. Baulieu expired, taking his secret with him. This happened in 1648.

The child was then seven years old. His charming manners grew with his age, and the count and countess felt their love for him increase. They caused him to be taught dancing and fencing, put him into breeches and hose, and a page's suit of their livery, in which capacity he served them. The marquis turned his attack to this quarter. He was doubtless preparing some plot as criminal as the preceding, when justice overtook him for some other great crimes of which he had been guilty. He was arrested one day in the street when conversing with one of the Saint-Geran footmen, and taken to the Conciergerie of the Palace of Justice.

Whether owing to these occurrences, or to grounds for suspicion before mentioned, certain reports spread in the Bourbonnais embodying some of the real facts; portions of them reached the ears of the count and countess, but they had only the effect of renewing their grief without furnishing a clue to the truth.

Meanwhile, the count went to take the waters at Vichy. The countess and Madame de Bouille followed him, and there they chanced to encounter Louise Goillard, the midwife. This woman renewed her acquaintance with the house, and in particular often visited the Marchioness de Bouille. One day the countess, unexpectedly entering the marchioness's room, found them both conversing in an undertone. They stopped talking immediately, and appeared disconcerted.

The countess noticed this without attaching any importance to it, and asked the subject of their conversation.

'Oh, nothing,' said the marchioness.

'But what is it?' insisted the countess, seeing that she blushed.

The marchioness, no longer able to evade the question, and feeling her difficulties increase, replied—

'Dame Louise is praising my brother for bearing no ill-will to her.'

'Why?' said the countess, turning to the midwife. 'Why should you fear any ill-will on the part of my husband?'

'I was afraid,' said Louise Goillard awkwardly, 'that he might have taken a dislike to me on account of all that happened when you expected to be confined.'

The obscurity of these words and embarrassment of the two women produced a lively effect upon the countess; but she controlled herself and let the subject drop. Her agitation, however, did not escape the notice of the marchioness, who the next day had horses put to her coach and retired to her estate of Lavoine. This clumsy proceeding strengthened suspicion.

The first determination of the countess was to arrest Louise Goillard; but she saw that in so serious a matter every step must be taken with precaution. She consulted the count and the countess dowager. They quietly summoned the midwife, to question her without any preliminaries. She prevaricated and contradicted herself over and over again; moreover, her state of terror alone sufficed to convict her of a crime. They handed her over to the law, and the Count de Saint-Geran filed an information before the vice-seneschal of Moulins.

The midwife underwent a first interrogatory. She confessed the truth of the accouchement, but she added that the countess had given birth to a still-born daughter, which she had buried under a stone near the step of the barn in the back yard. The judge, accompanied by a physician and a surgeon, repaired to the place, where he found neither stone, nor foetus, nor any indications of an interment. They searched unsuccessfully in other places.

When the dowager countess heard this statement, she demanded that this horrible woman should be put on her trial. The civil lieutenant, in the absence of the criminal lieutenant, commenced the proceedings.

In a second interrogation, Louise Goillard positively declared that the countess had never been confined;

In a third, that she had been delivered of a mole;

In a fourth, that she had been confined of a male infant, which Baulieu had carried away in a basket;

And in a fifth, in which she answered from the dock, she maintained that her evidence of the countess's accouchement had been extorted from her by violence. She made no charges against either Madame de Bouille or the Marquis de Saint-Maixent. On the other hand, no sooner was she under lock and key than she despatched her son Guillemin to the marchioness to inform her that she was arrested. The marchioness recognised how threatening things were, and was in a state of consternation; she immediately sent the sieur de la Foresterie, her steward, to the lieutenant-general, her counsel, a mortal enemy of the count, that he might advise her in this conjuncture, and suggest a means for helping the matron without appearing openly in the matter. The lieutenant's advice was to quash the proceedings and obtain an injunction against the continuance of the preliminaries to the action. The marchioness spent a large sum of money, and obtained this injunction; but it was immediately reversed, and the bar to the suit removed.

La Foresterie was then ordered to pass to Riom, where the

sisters Quinet lived, and to bribe them heavily to secrecy. The elder one, on leaving the marchioness's service, had shaken her fist in her face, feeling secure with the secrets in her knowledge, and told her that she would repent having dismissed her and her sister, and that she would make a clean breast of the whole affair, even were she to be hung first. These girls then sent word that they wished to enter her service again; that the countess had promised them handsome terms if they would speak; and that they had even been questioned in her name by a Capuchin superior, but that they said nothing, in order to give time to prepare an answer for them. The marchioness found herself obliged to take back the girls; she kept the younger, and married the elder to Delisle, her house steward. But la Foresterie, finding himself in this network of intrigue, grew disgusted at serving such a mistress, and left her house. The marchioness told him on his departure that if he were so indiscreet as to repeat a word of what he had learned from the Quinet girls, she would punish him with a hundred poniard stabs from her major-domo Delisle. Having thus fortified her position, she thought herself secure against any hostile steps; but it happened that a certain prudent Berger, gentleman and page to the Marquis de Saint-Maixent, who enjoyed his master's confidence and went to see him in the Conciergerie, where he was imprisoned, threw some strange light on this affair. His master had narrated to him all the particulars of the accouchement of the countess and of the abduction of the child.

'I am astonished, my lord,' replied the page, 'that having so many dangerous affairs on hand; you did not relieve your conscience of this one.'

'I intend,' replied the marquis, 'to restore this child to his father: I have been ordered to do so by a Capuchin to whom I confessed having carried off from the midst of the family, without their knowing it, a grandson of a marshal of France and son of a governor of a province.'

The marquis had at that time permission to go out from prison occasionally on his parole. This will not surprise anyone acquainted with the ideas which prevailed at that period on the honour of a nobleman, even the greatest criminal. The marquis, profiting by this facility, took the page to see a child of about seven years of age, fair and with a beautiful countenance.

'Page,' said he, 'look well at this child, so that you may know him again when I shall send you to inquire about him.'

He then informed him that this was the Count de Saint-Geran's son whom he had carried away.

Information of these matters coming to the ears of justice, decisive proofs were hoped for; but this happened just when other criminal informations were lodged against the marquis, which left him helpless to prevent the exposure of his crimes. Police officers were despatched in all haste to the Conciergerie; they were stopped by the gaolers, who told them that the marquis, feeling ill, was engaged with a priest who was administering the sacraments to him. As they insisted on seeing him, the warders approached the cell: the priest came out, crying that persons must be sought to whom the sick man had a secret to reveal; that he was in a desperate state, and said he had just poisoned himself; all entered the cell.

M. de Saint-Maixent was writhing on a pallet, in a pitiable condition, sometimes shrieking like a wild beast, sometimes stammering disconnected words. All that the officers could hear was—

'Monsieur le Comte...call...the Countess...de Saint-Geran ...let them come...' The officers earnestly begged him to try to be more explicit.

The marquis had another fit; when he opened his eyes, he said—

'Send for the countess...let them forgive me...I wish to tell them everything.' The police officers asked him to speak; one even told him that the count was there. The marquis feebly murmured—

'I am going to tell you—' Then he gave a loud cry and fell back dead.

It thus seemed as if fate took pains to close every mouth from which the truth might escape. Still, this avowal of a deathbed revelation to be made to the Count de Saint-Geran and the deposition of the priest who had administered the last sacraments formed a strong link in the chain of evidence.

The judge of first instruction, collecting all the information he had got, made a report the weight of which was overwhelming. The carters, the nurse, the domestic servants, all gave accounts consistent with each other; the route and the various adventures of the child were plainly detailed, from its birth till its arrival at the village of Descoutoux.

Justice, thus tracing crime to its sources, had no option but to issue a warrant for the arrest of the Marchioness de Bouille; but it seems probable that it was not served owing to the strenuous efforts of the Count de Saint-Geran, who could not bring himself to ruin his sister, seeing that her dishonour would have been reflected on him. The marchioness hid her remorse in solitude, and appeared again no more. She died shortly after, carrying the weight of her secret till she drew her last breath.

The judge of Moulins at length pronounced sentence on the midwife, whom he declared arraigned and convicted of having suppressed the child born to the countess; for which he condemned her to be tortured and then hanged. The matron lodged an appeal against this sentence, and the case was referred to the Conciergerie.

No sooner had the count and countess seen the successive proofs of the procedure, than tenderness and natural feelings accomplished the rest. They no longer doubted that their page was their son; they stripped him at once of his livery and gave him his rank and prerogatives, under the title of the Count de la Palice.

Meanwhile, a private person named Sequeville informed the countess that he had made a very important discovery; that a child had been baptized in 1642 at St. Jean-en-Greve, and that a woman named Marie Pigoreau had taken a leading part in the affair. Thereupon inquiries were made, and it was discovered that this child had been nursed in the village of Torcy. The count obtained a warrant which enabled him to get evidence before the judge of Torcy; nothing was left undone to elicit the whole truth; he also obtained a warrant through which he obtained more information, and published a monitory. The elder of the Quinet girls on this told the Marquis de Canillac that the count was searching at a distance for things very near him. The truth shone out with great lustre through these new facts which gushed from all this fresh information. The child, exhibited in the presence of a legal commissary to the nurses and witnesses of Torcy, was identified, as much by the scars left by the midwife's nails on his head, as by his fair hair and blue eyes. This ineffaceable vestige of the woman's cruelty was the principal proof; the witnesses testified that la Pigoreau, when she visited this child with a man who appeared to be of condition, always asserted that he was the son of a great nobleman who had been entrusted to her care, and that she hoped he would make her fortune and that of those who had reared him.

The child's godfather, Paul Marmiou, a common labourer; the grocer Raguenet, who had charge of the two thousand livres; the servant of la Pigoreau, who had heard her say that the count was obliged to take this child; the witnesses who proved that la Pigoreau had told them that the child was too well born to wear a page's livery, all furnished convincing proofs; but others were forthcoming.

It was at la Pigoreau's that the Marquis de Saint-Maixent, living then at the hotel de Saint-Geran, went to see the child, kept in her house as if it were hers. Prudent Berger, the marquis's page, perfectly well remembered la Pigoreau, and also the child, whom he had seen at her house and whose history the marquis had related to him. Finally, many other witnesses heard in the course of the case, both before the three chambers of nobles, clergy, and the tiers etat, and before the judges of Torcy, Cusset, and other local magistrates, made the facts so clear and conclusive in favour of the legitimacy of the young count, that it was impossible to avoid impeaching the guilty parties. The count ordered the summons in person of la Pigoreau, who had not been compromised in the original preliminary proceedings. This drastic measure threw the intriguing woman on her beam ends, but she strove hard to right herself.

The widowed Duchess de Ventadour, daughter by her mother's second marriage of the Countess dowager of Saint-Geran, and half-sister of the count, and the Countess de Lude, daughter of the Marchioness de Bouille, from whom the young count carried away the Saint-Geran inheritance, were very warm in the matter, and spoke of disputing the judgment. La Pigoreau went to see them, and joined in concert with them.

Then commenced this famous lawsuit, which long occupied all France, and is parallel in some respects, but not in the time occupied in the hearing, to the case heard by Solomon, in which one child was claimed by two mothers.

The Marquis de Saint-Maixent and Madame de Bouille being dead, were naturally no parties to the suit, which was fought against the Saint-Geran family by la Pigoreau and Mesdames du Lude and de Ventadour. These ladies no doubt acted in good faith, at first at any rate, in refusing to believe the crime; for if they had originally known the truth it is incredible that they could have fought the case so long and so obstinately.

They first of all went to the aid of the midwife, who had fallen sick in prison; they then consulted together, and resolved as follows:

That the accused should appeal against criminal proceedings;

That la Pigoreau should lodge a civil petition against the judgments which ordered her arrest and the confronting of witnesses;

That they should appeal against the abuse of obtaining and publishing monitories, and lodge an interpleader against the sentence of the judge of first instruction, who had condemned the matron to capital punishment;

And that finally, to carry the war into the enemy's camp, la Pigoreau should impugn the maternity of the countess, claiming the child as her own; and that the ladies should depose that the countess's accouchement was an imposture invented to cause it to be supposed that she had given birth to a child.

For more safety and apparent absence of collusion, Mesdames du Lude and de Ventadour pretended to have no communication with la Pigoreau.

About this time the midwife died in prison, from an illness which vexation and remorse had aggravated. After her death, her son Guillemin confessed that she had often told him that the countess had given birth to a son whom Baulieu had carried off, and that the child entrusted to Baulieu at the chateau Saint-Geran was the same as the one recovered; the youth added that he had concealed this fact so long as it might injure his mother, and he further stated that the ladies de Ventadour and du Lude had helped her in prison with money and advice—another strong piece of presumptive evidence.

The petitions of the accused and the interpleadings of Mesdames du Lude and de Ventadour were discussed in seven hearings, before three courts convened. The suit proceeded with all the languor and chicanery of the period.

After long and specious arguments, the attorney general Bijnon gave his decision in favour of the Count and Countess of Saint-Geran, concluding thus:—

'The court rejects the civil appeal of la Pigoreau; and all the opposition and appeals of the appellants and the defendants; condemns them to fine and in costs; and seeing that the charges against la Pigoreau were of a serious nature, and that a personal summons had been decreed against her, orders her committal, recommending her to the indulgence of the court.'

By a judgment given in a sitting at the Tournelle by M. de Mesmes, on the 18th of August 1657, the appellant ladies' and the defendants' opposition was rejected with fine and costs. La Pigoreau was forbidden to leave the city and suburbs of Paris under penalty of summary conviction. The judgment in the case followed the rejection of the appeal.

This reverse at first extinguished the litigation of Mesdames du Lude and de Ventadour, but it soon revived more briskly than ever. These ladies, who had taken la Pigoreau in their coach to all the hearings, prompted her, in order to procrastinate, to file a fresh petition, in which she demanded the confrontment of all the witnesses to the pregnancy, and the confinement. On hearing this petition, the court gave on the 28th of August 1658 a decree ordering the confrontment, but on condition that for three days previously la Pigoreau should deliver herself a prisoner in the Conciergerie.

This judgment, the consequences of which greatly alarmed la Pigoreau, produced such an effect upon her that, after having weighed the interest she had in the suit, which she would lose by flight, against the danger to her life if she ventured her person into the hands of justice, she abandoned her false plea of maternity, and took refuge abroad. This last circumstance was a heavy blow to Mesdames du Lude and de

Ventadour; but they were not at the end of their resources and their obstinacy.

Contempt of court being decreed against la Pigoreau, and the case being got up against the other defendants, the Count de Saint-Geran left for the Bourbonnais, to put in execution the order to confront the witnesses. Scarcely had he arrived in the province when he was obliged to interrupt his work to receive the king and the queen mother, who were returning from Lyons and passing through Moulins. He presented the Count de la Palice to their Majesties as his son; they received him as such. But during the visit of the king and queen the Count de Saint-Geran fell ill, over fatigued, no doubt, by the trouble he had taken to give them a suitable reception, over and above the worry of his own affairs.

During his illness, which only lasted a week, he made in his will a new acknowledgment of his son, naming his executors M. de Barriere, intendant of the province, and the sieur Vialet, treasurer of France, desiring them to bring the lawsuit to an end. His last words were for his wife and child; his only regret that he had not been able to terminate this affair. He died on the 31st of January 1659.

The maternal tenderness of the countess did not need stimulating by the injunctions of her husband, and she took up the suit with energy. The ladies de Ventadour and du Lude obtained by default letters of administration as heiresses without liability, which were granted out of the Chatelet. At the same time they appealed against the judgment of the lieutenant-general of the Bourbonnais, giving the tutelage of the young count to the countess his mother, and his guardianship to sieur de Bompre. The countess, on her side, interpleaded an appeal against the granting of letters of administration without liability, and did all in her power to bring back the case to the Tournelle. The other ladies carried their appeal to the high court, pleading that they were not parties to the lawsuit in the Tournelle.

It would serve no purpose to follow the obscure labyrinth of legal procedure of that period, and to recite all the marches and countermarches which legal subtlety suggested to the litigants. At the end of three years, on the 9th of April 1661, the countess obtained a judgment by which the king in person—

> 'Assuming to his own decision the civil suit pending at the Tournelle, as well as the appeals pled by both parties, and the last petition of Mesdames du Lude and de Ventadour, sends back the whole case to the three assembled chambers of the States General, to be by them decided on its merits either jointly or separately, as they may deem fit.'

The countess thus returned to her first battlefield. Legal science produced an immense quantity of manuscript, barristers and attorneys greatly distinguishing themselves in their calling. After an interminable hearing, and pleadings longer and more complicated than ever, which however did not bamboozle the court, judgment was pronounced in conformity with the summing up of the attorney-general, thus—

'That passing over the petition of Mesdames Marie de la Guiche and Eleonore de Bouille, on the grounds,' etc. etc.;

'Evidence taken,' etc.;

'Appeals, judgments annulled,' etc.;

'With regard to the petition of the late Claude de la Guiche and Suzanne de Longaunay, dated 12th August 1658,'

'Ordered,

'That the rule be made absolute;

'Which being done, Bernard de la Guiche is pronounced, maintained, and declared the lawfully born and legitimate son of Claude de la Guiche and Suzanne de Longaunay; in possession and enjoyment of the name and arms of the house of Guiche, and of all the goods left by Claude de la Guiche, his father; and Marie de la Guiche and Eleonore de Bouille are interdicted from interfering with him;

'The petitions of Eleonore de Bouille and Marie de la Guiche, dated 4th June 1664, 4th August 1665, 6th January, 10th February, 12th March, 15th April, and 2nd June, 1666, are dismissed with costs;

'Declared,

'That the defaults against la Pigoreau are confirmed; and that she, arraigned and convicted of the offences imputed to her, is condemned to be hung and strangled at a gallows erected in the Place de Greve in this city, if taken and apprehended; otherwise, in effigy at a gallows erected in the Place de Greve aforesaid; that all her property subject to confiscation is seized and confiscated from whomsoever may be in possession of it; on which property and other not subject to confiscation, is levied a fine of eight hundred Paris livres, to be paid to the King, and applied to the maintenance of prisoners in the Conciergerie of the Palace of justice, and to the costs.'

Possibly a more obstinate legal contest was never waged, on both sides, but especially by those who lost it. The countess, who played the part of the true mother in the Bible, had the case so much to heart that she often told the judges, when pleading her cause, that if her son were not recognised as such, she would marry him, and convey all her property to him.

The young Count de la Palice became Count de Saint-Geran through the death of his father, married, in 1667, Claude Francoise Madeleine de Farignies, only daughter of Francois de Monfreville and of Marguerite Jourdain de Carbone de Canisi. He had only one daughter, born in 1688, who became a nun. He died at the age of fifty-five years, and thus this illustrious family became extinct.

ABOUT TERRY O'BRIEN

Terry O'Brien is an academic with three decades of experience in teaching language and communication skills in India and abroad. He also headed a college under the auspices of the University of Delhi.

A prolific writer, with several books to his credit, Terry O'Brien is a reputed professional motivational speaker and a quizmaster.